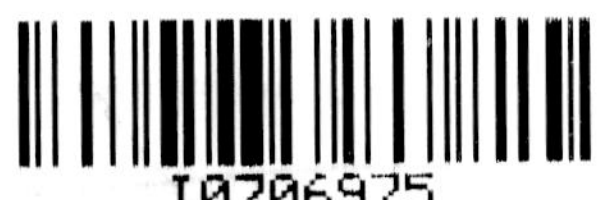

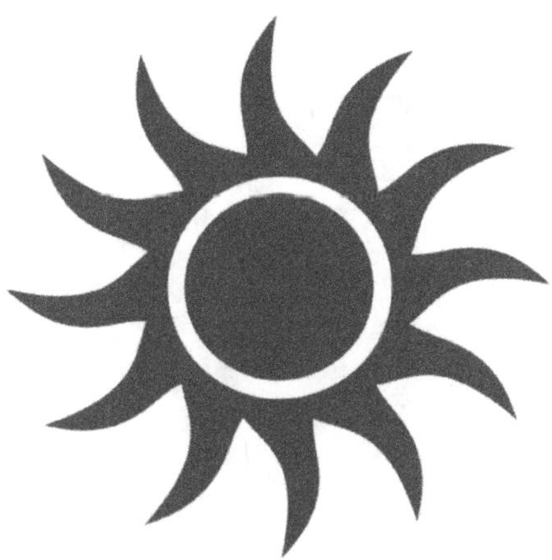

This Coloring Book Belongs To:

____

____

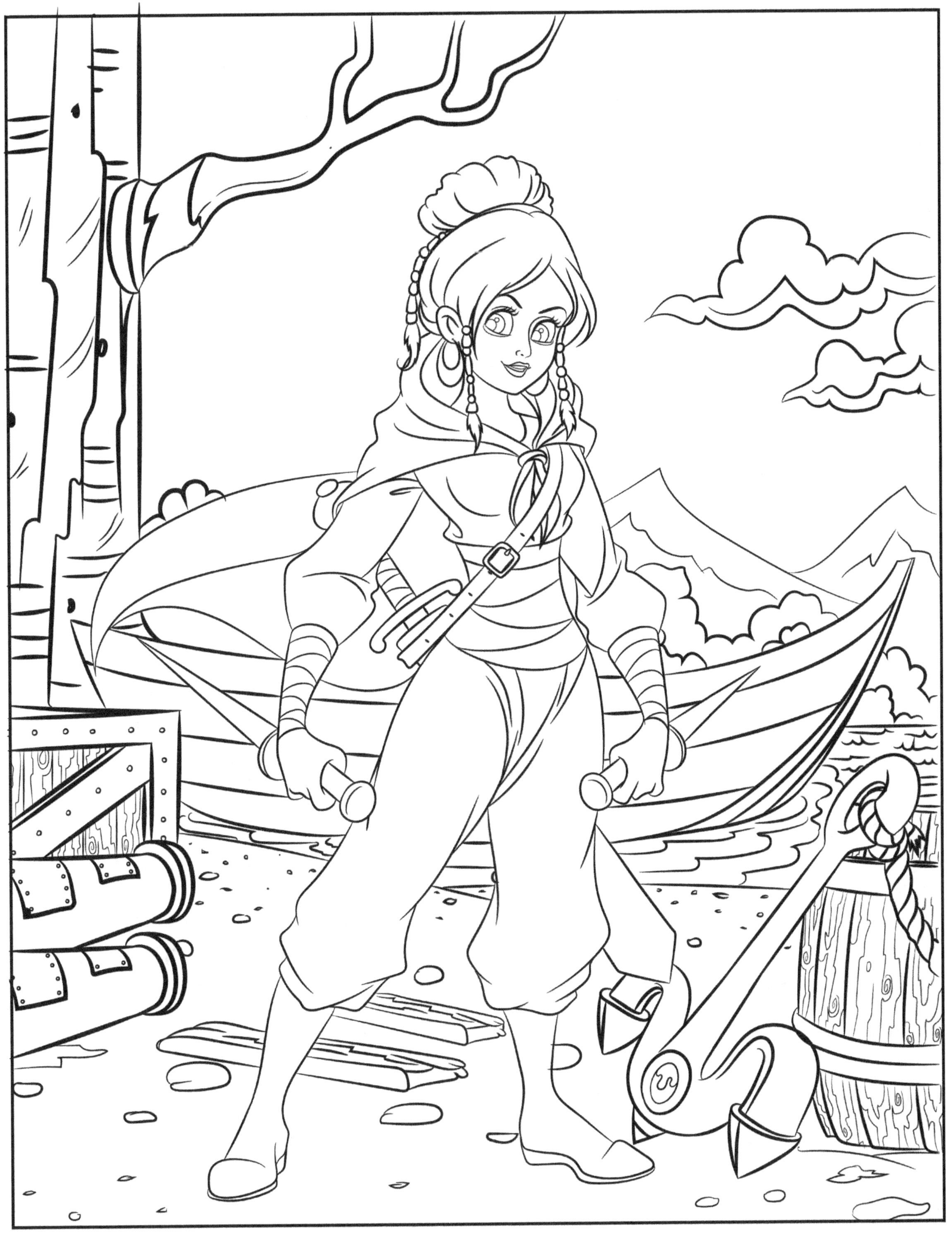

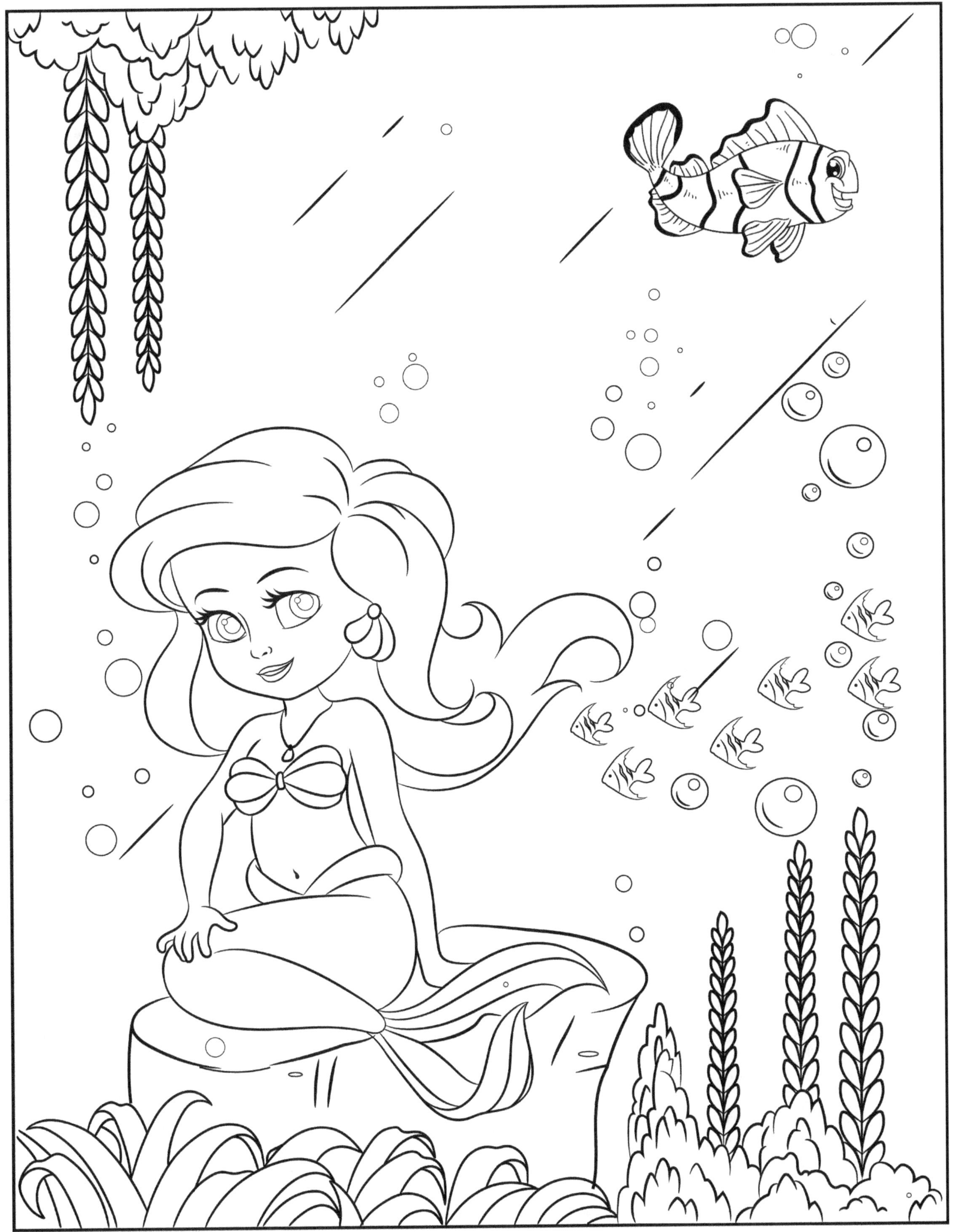

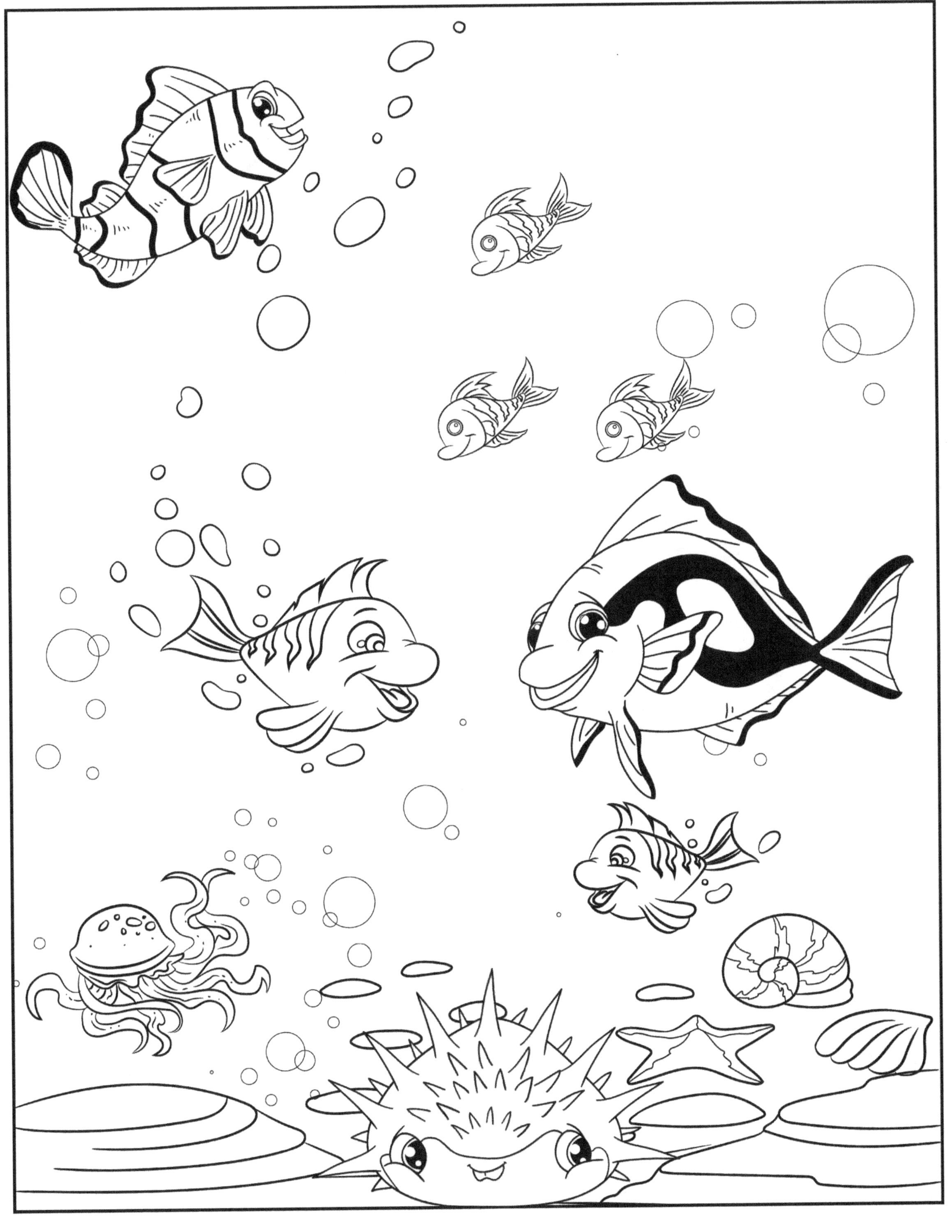

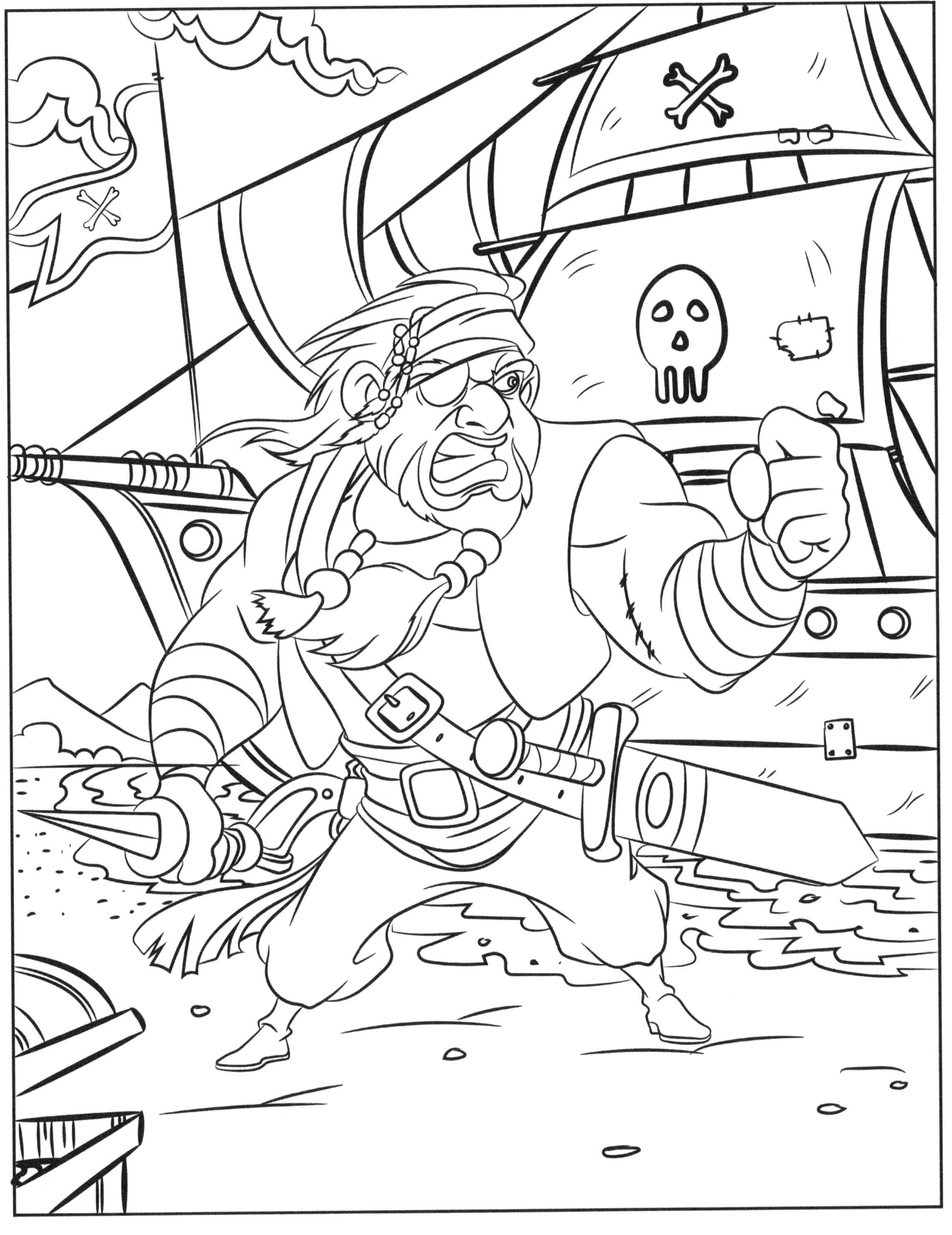

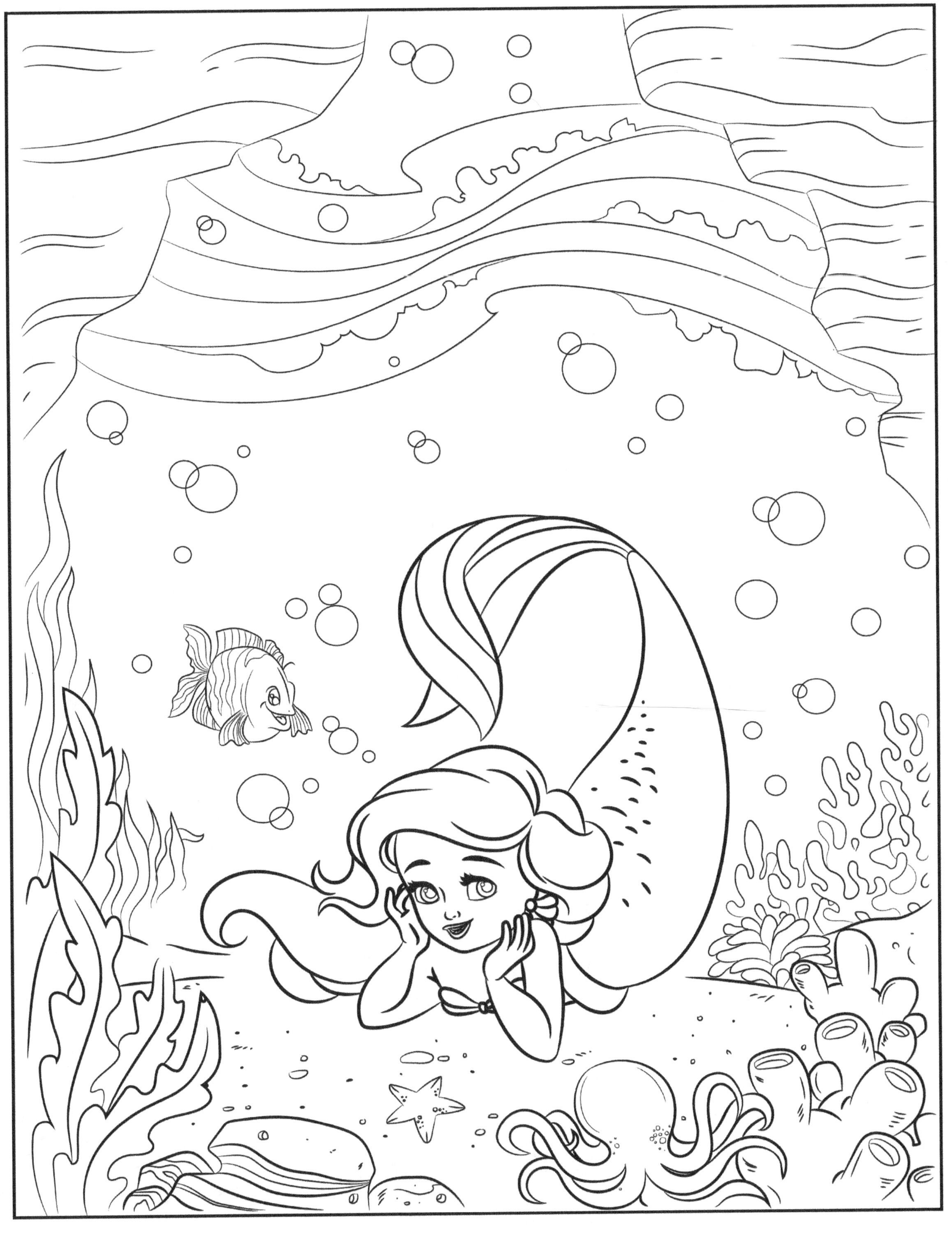

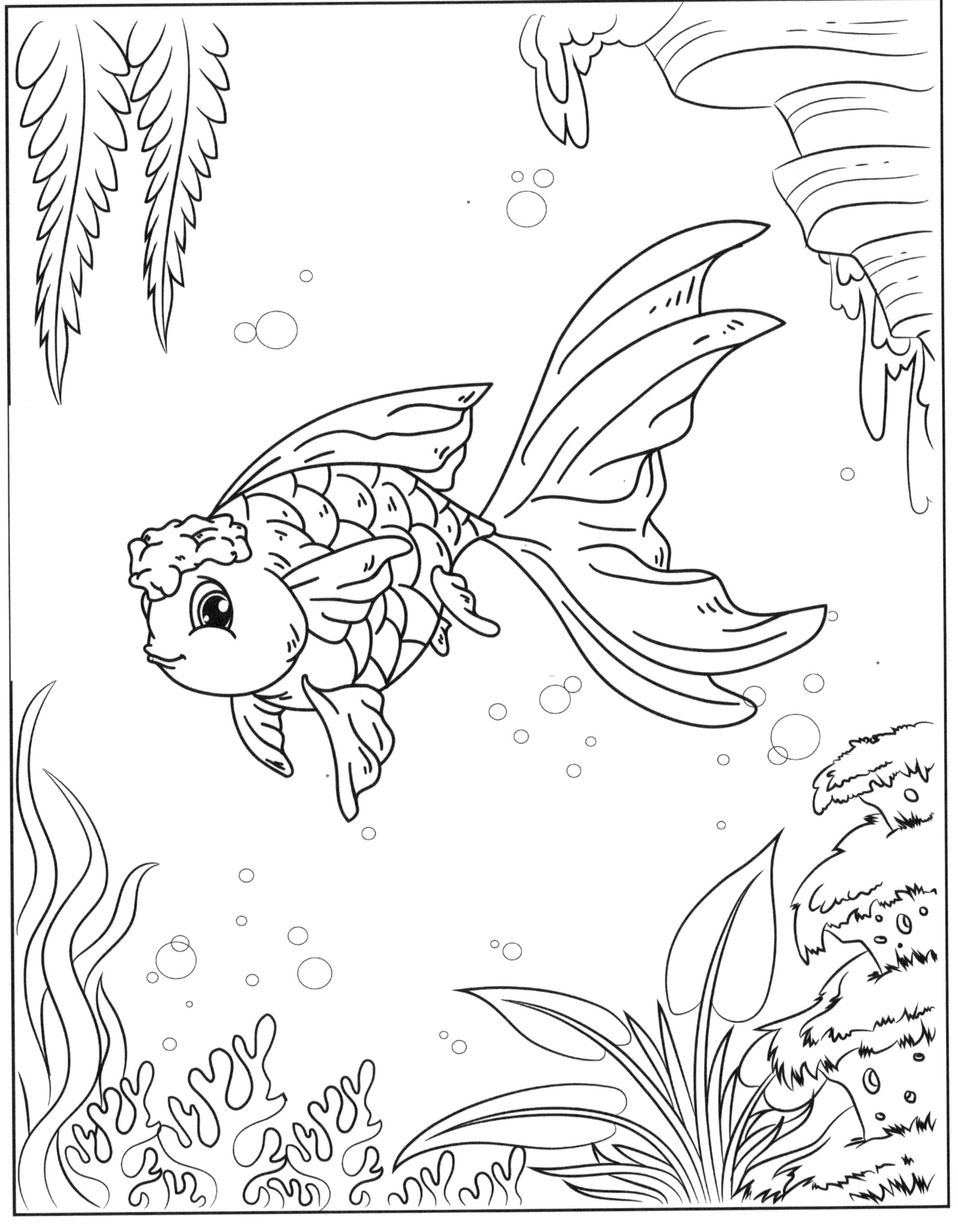

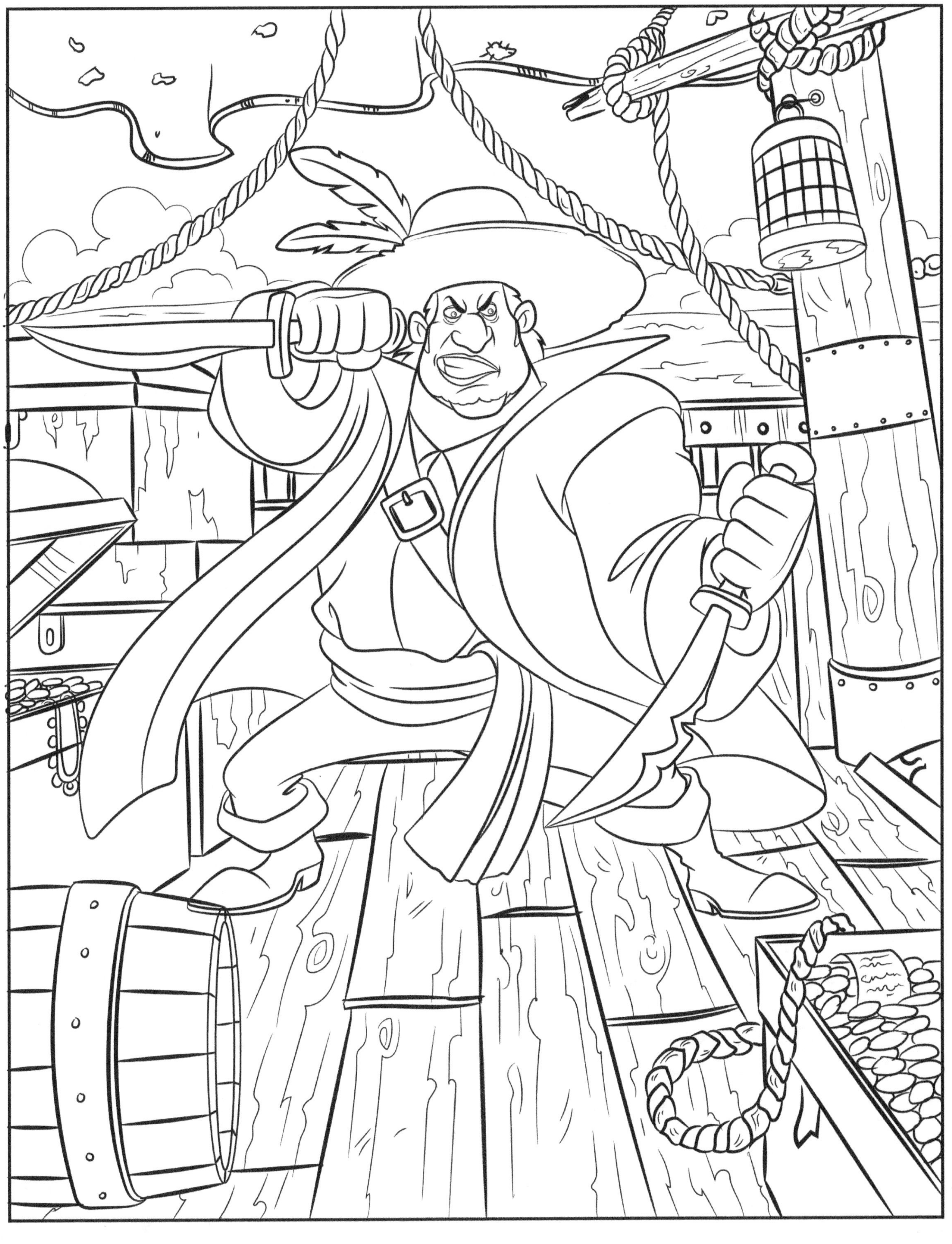

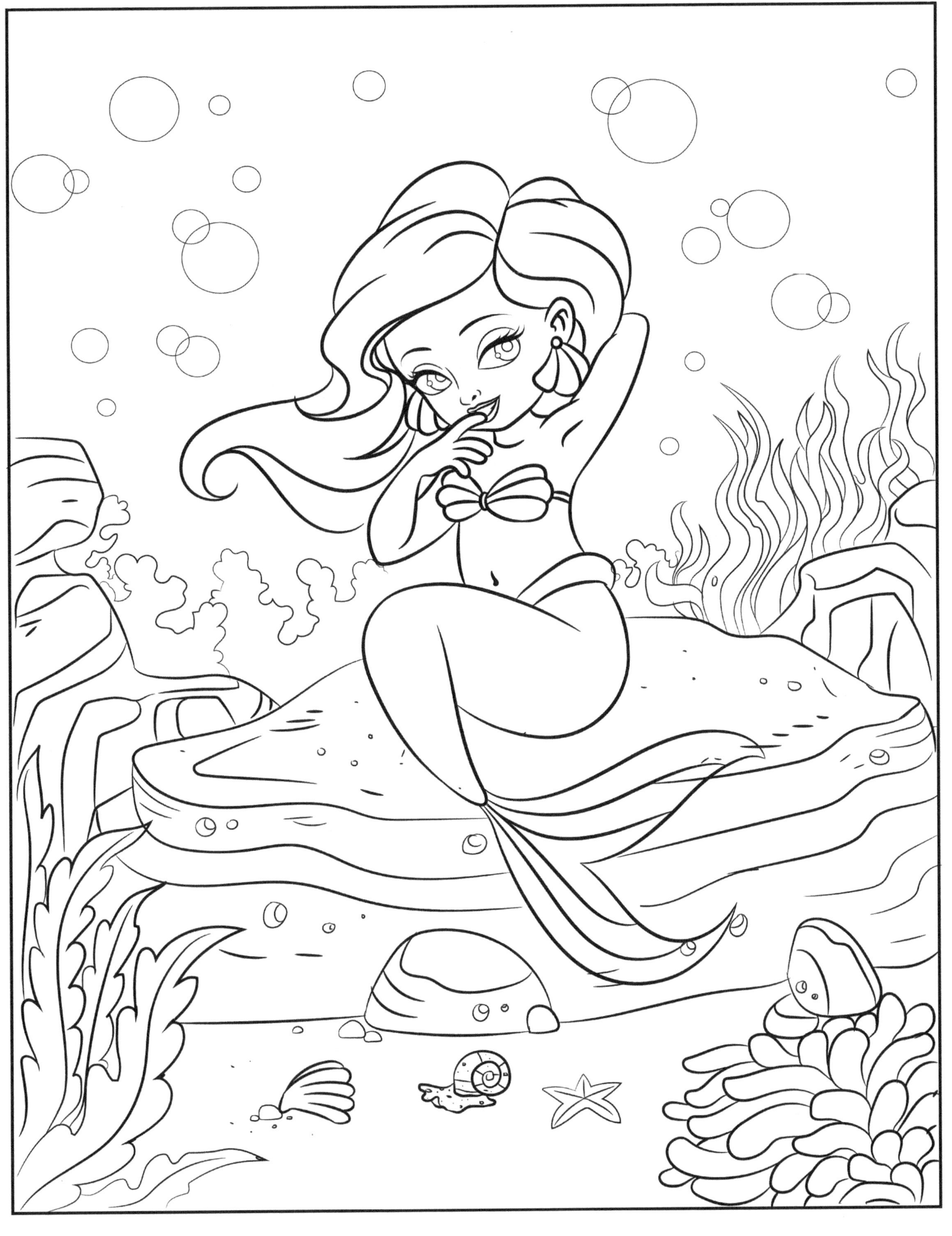

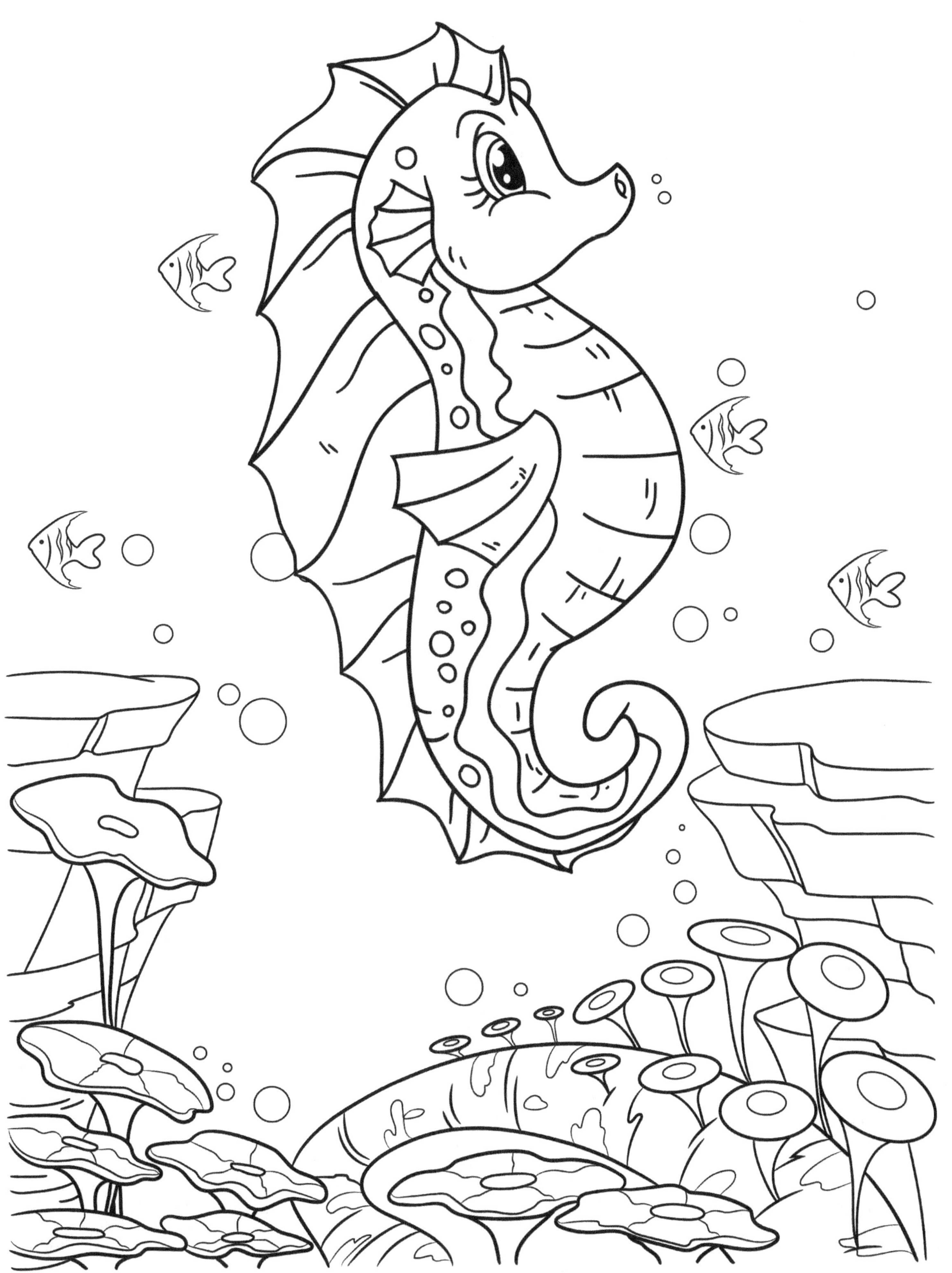

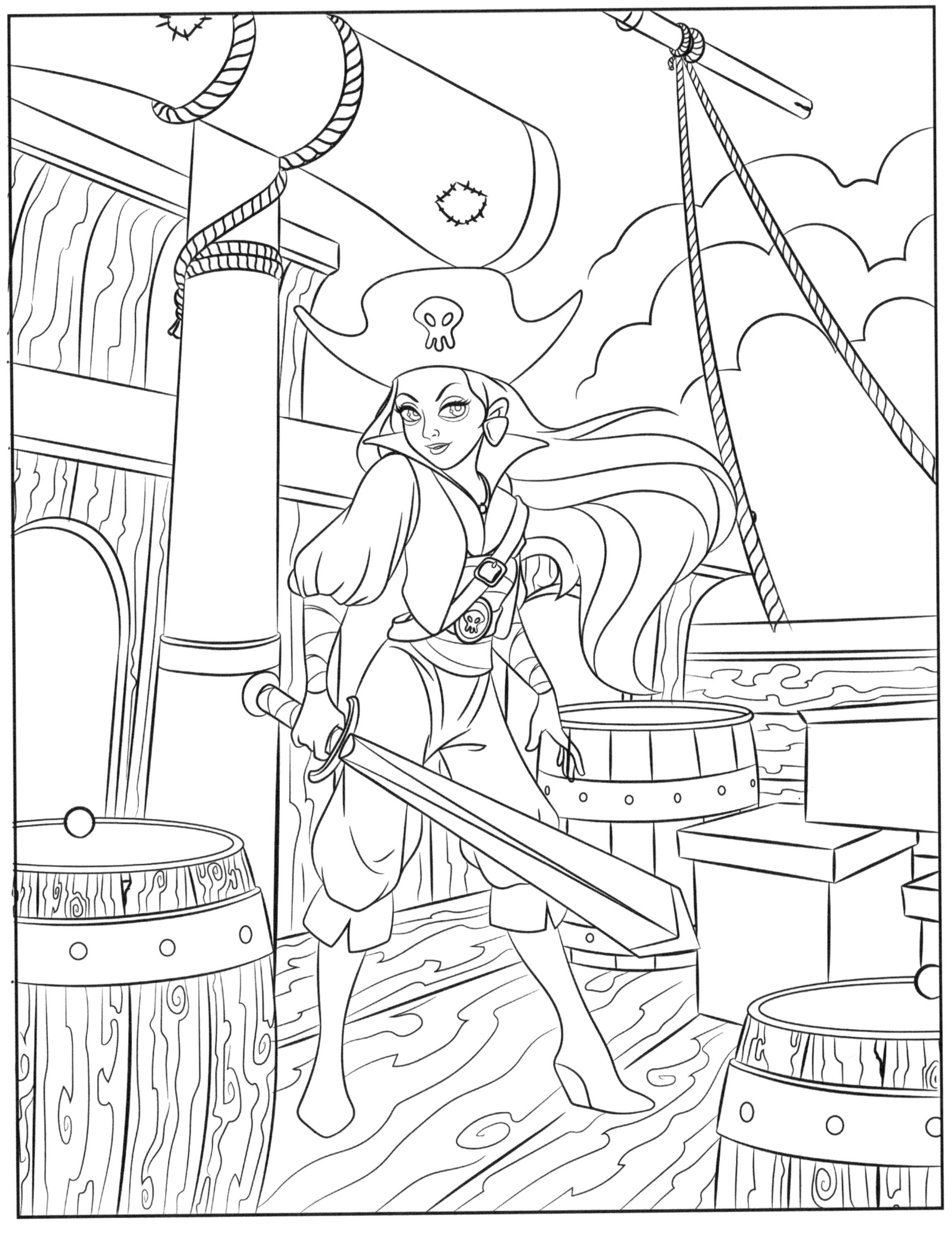

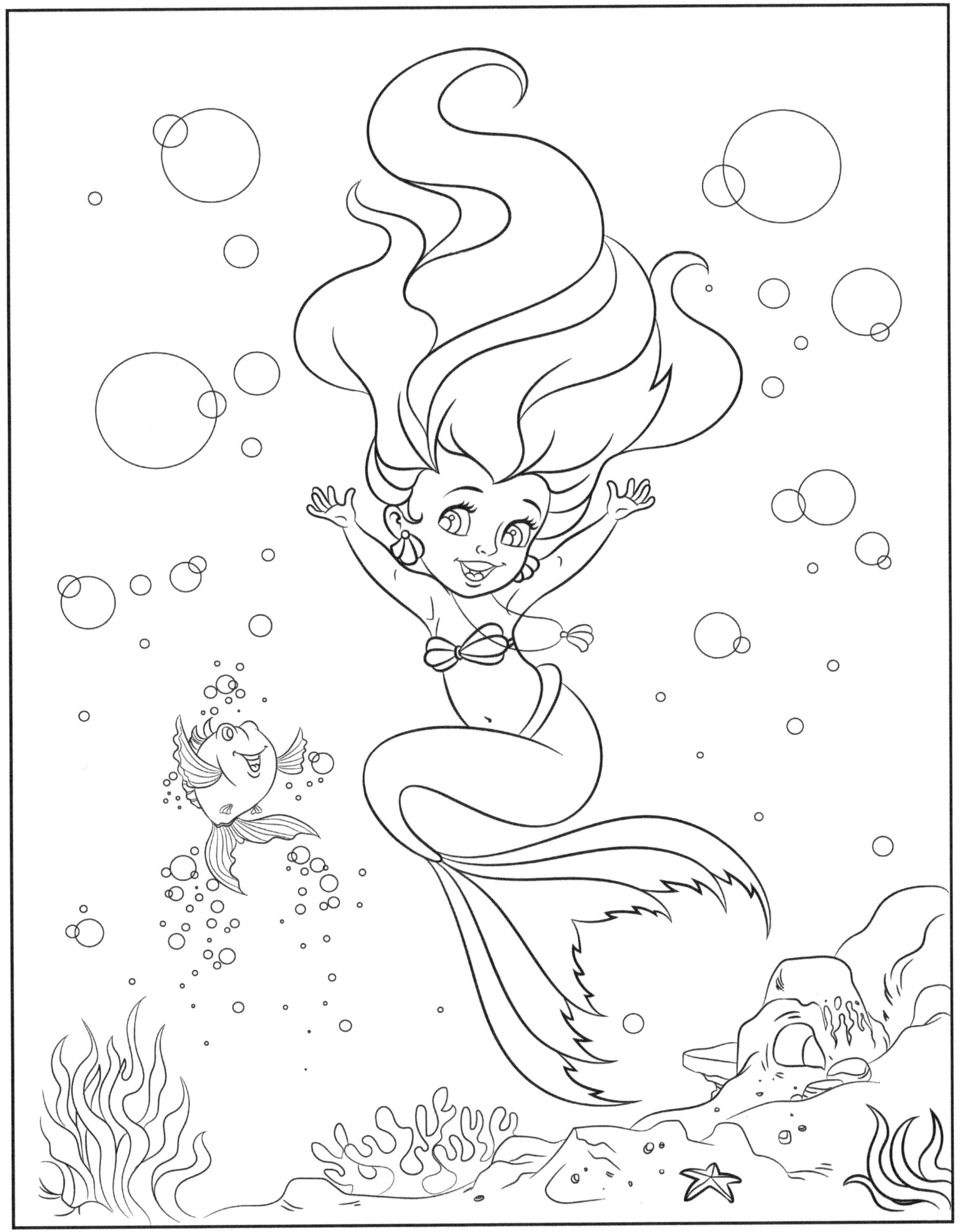

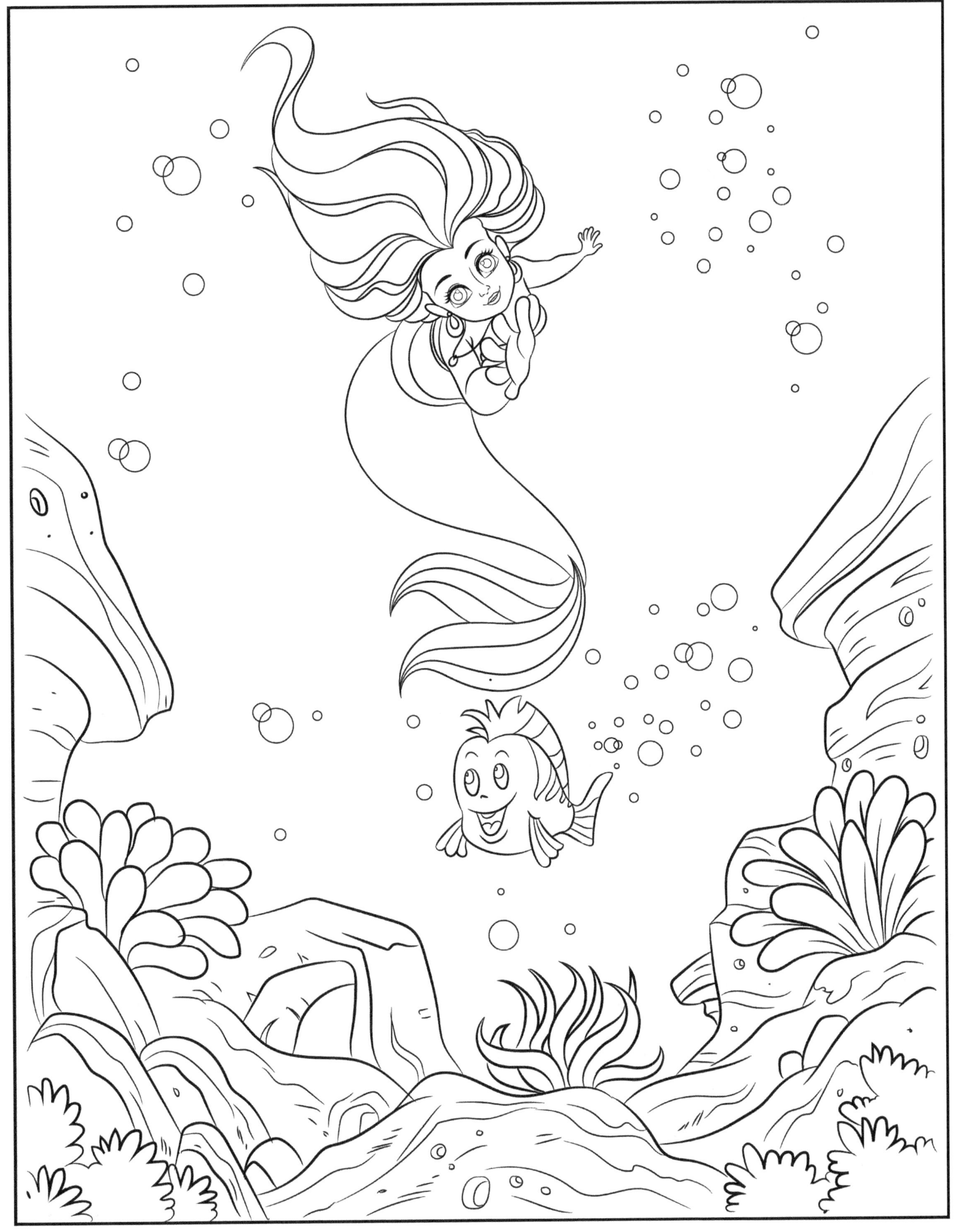

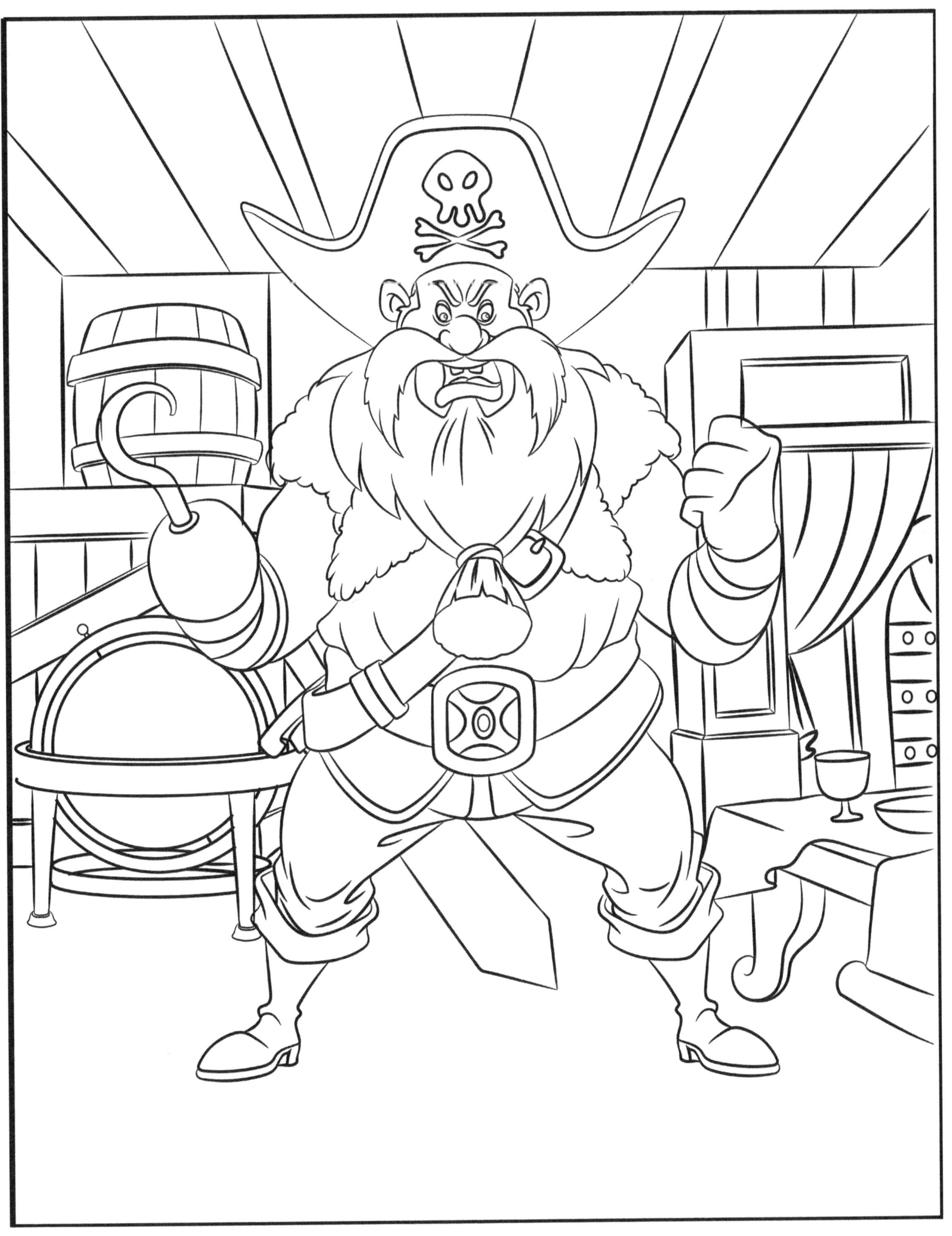

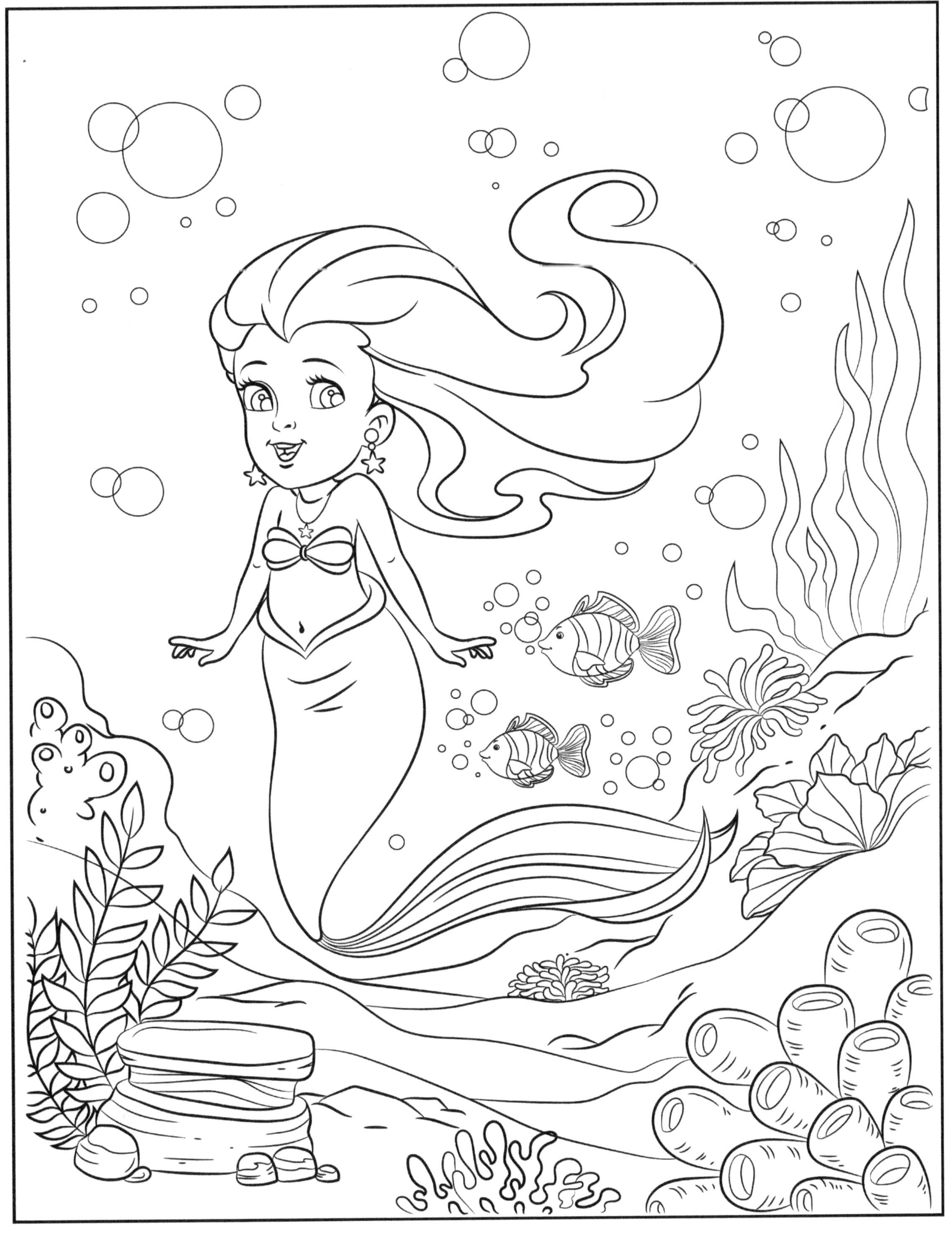

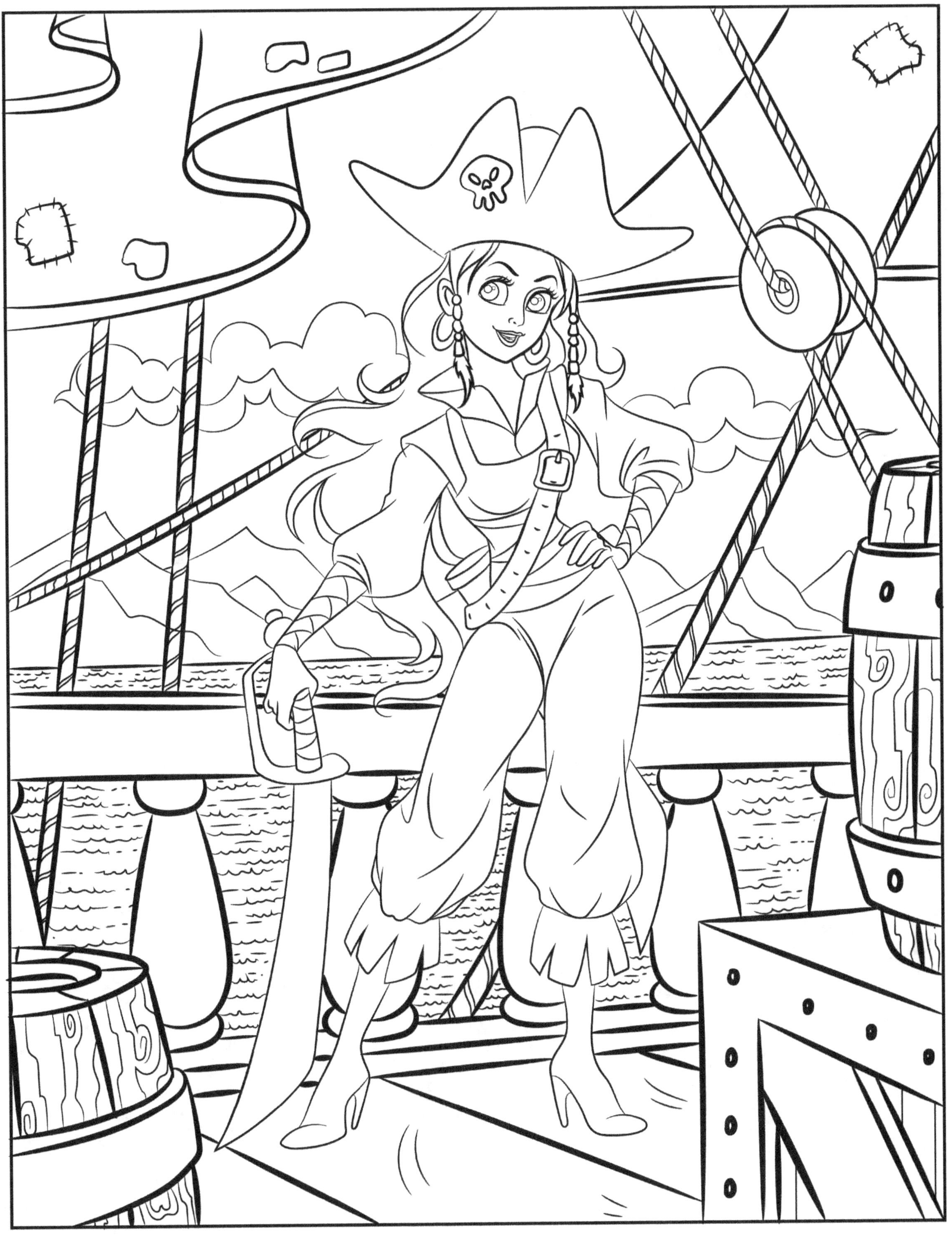

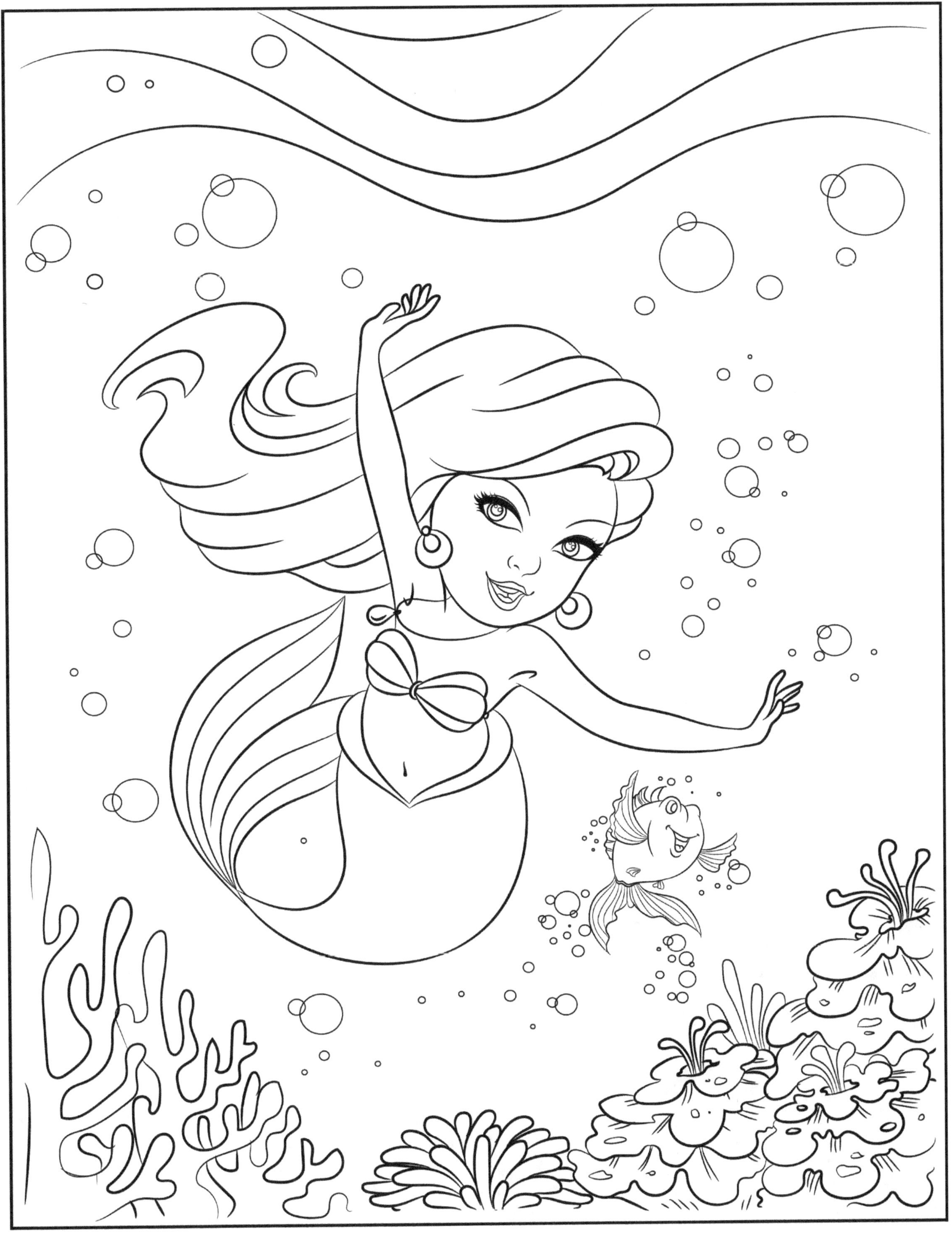

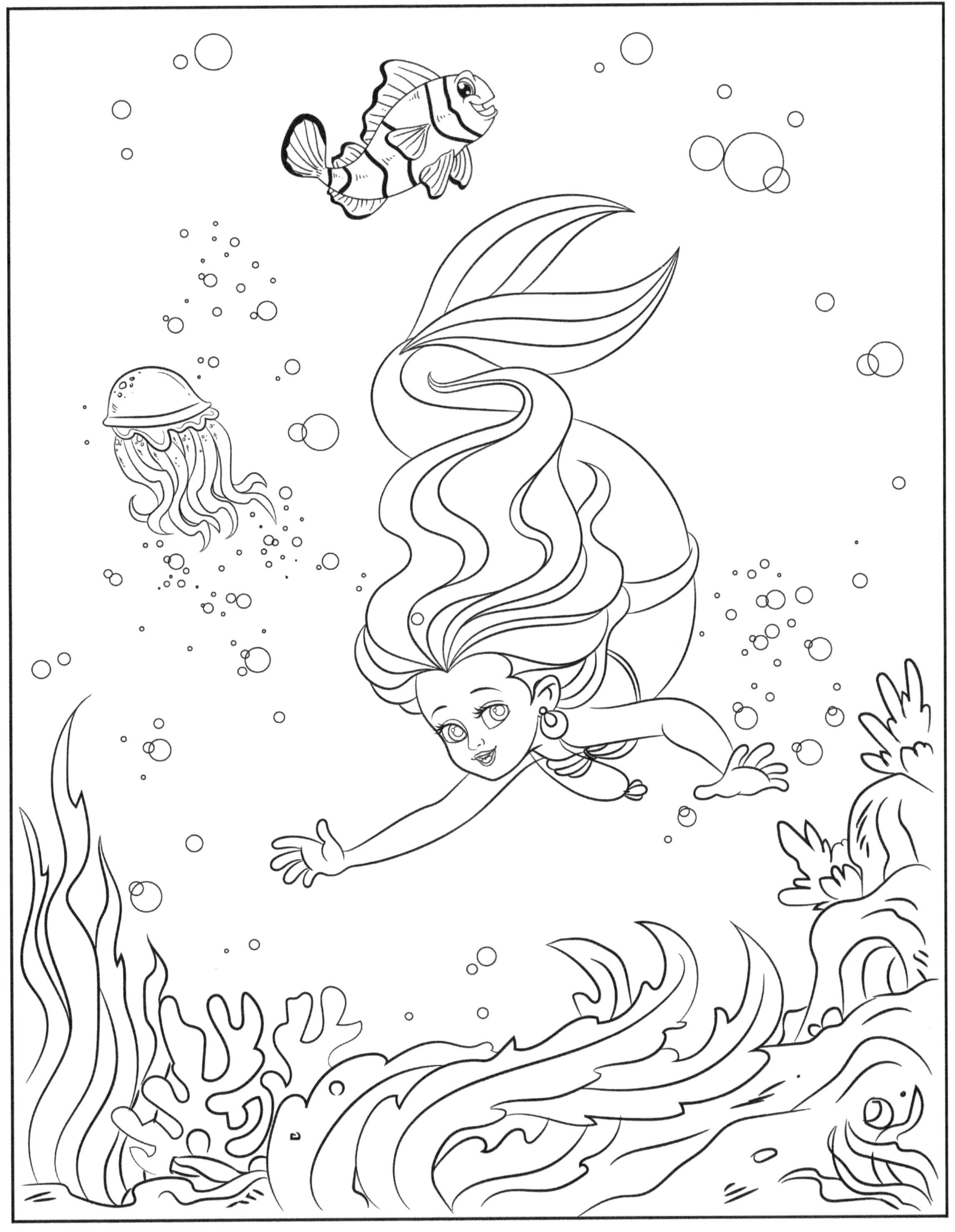

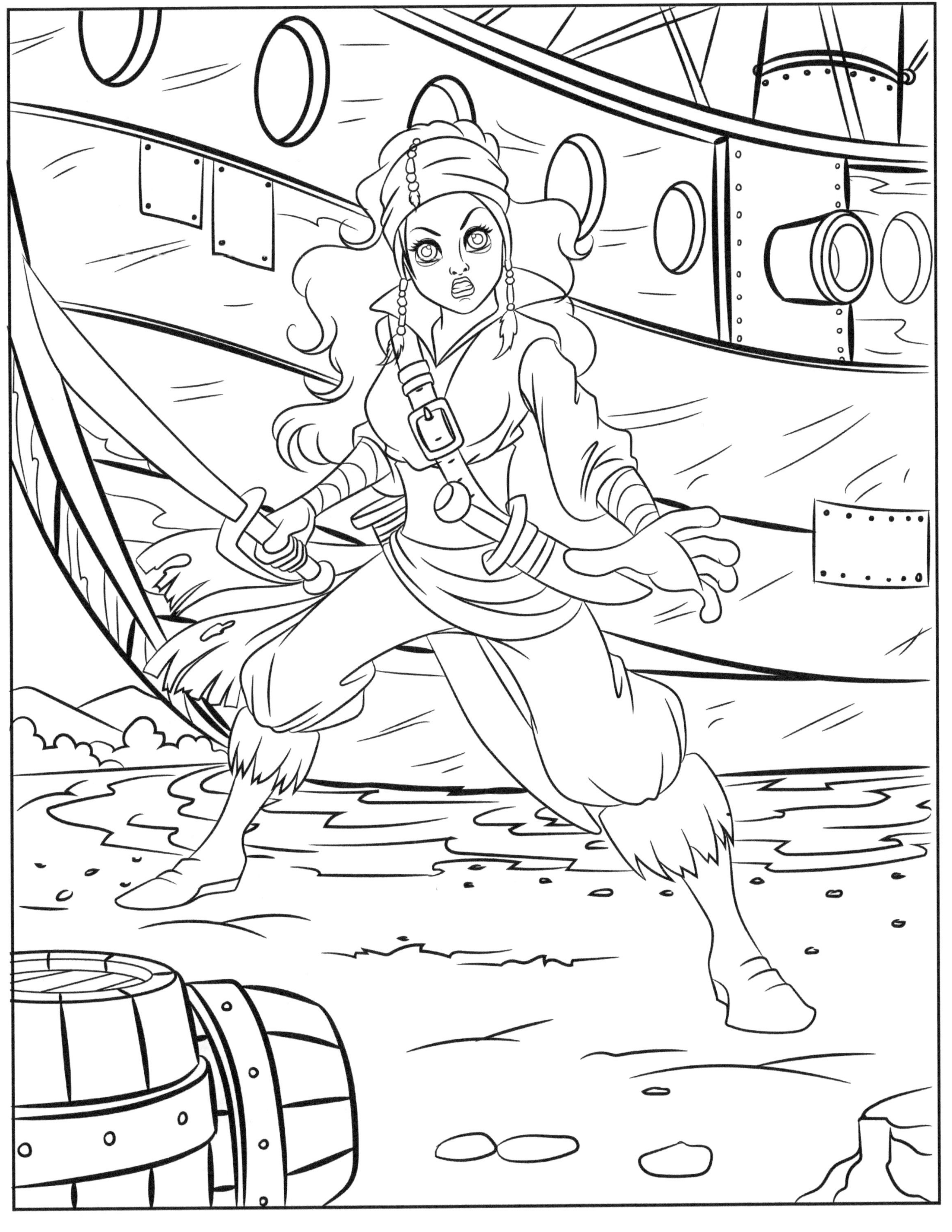

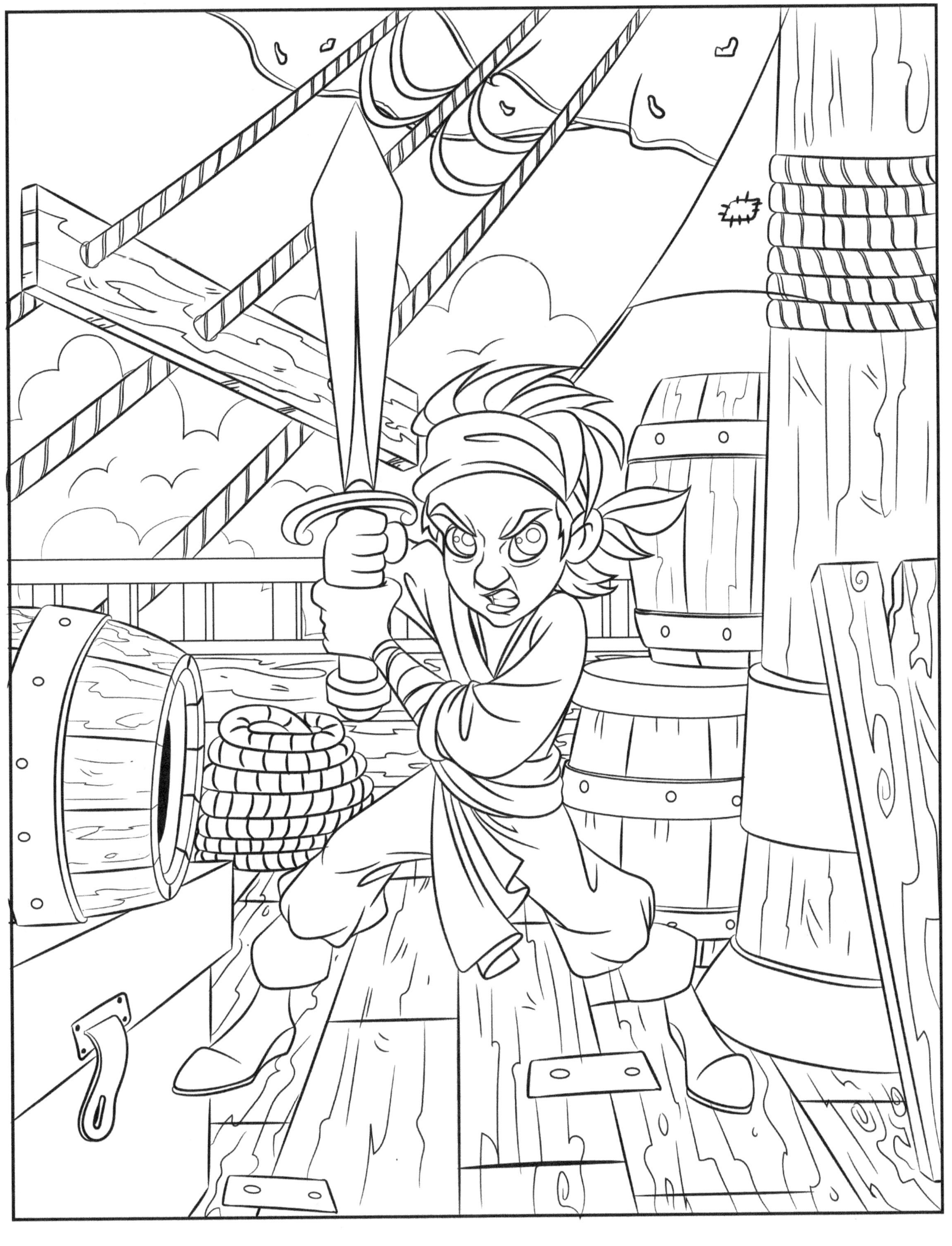

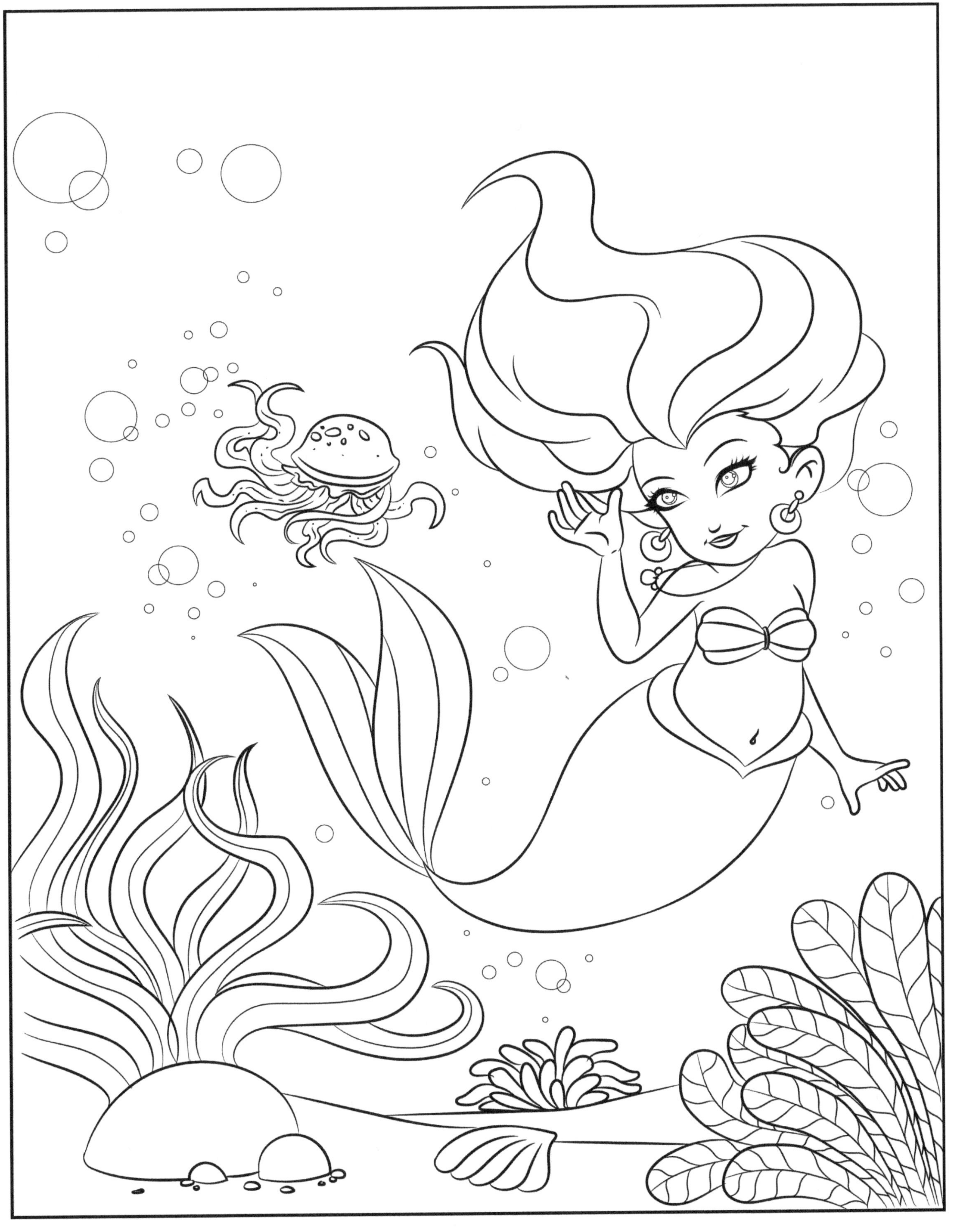

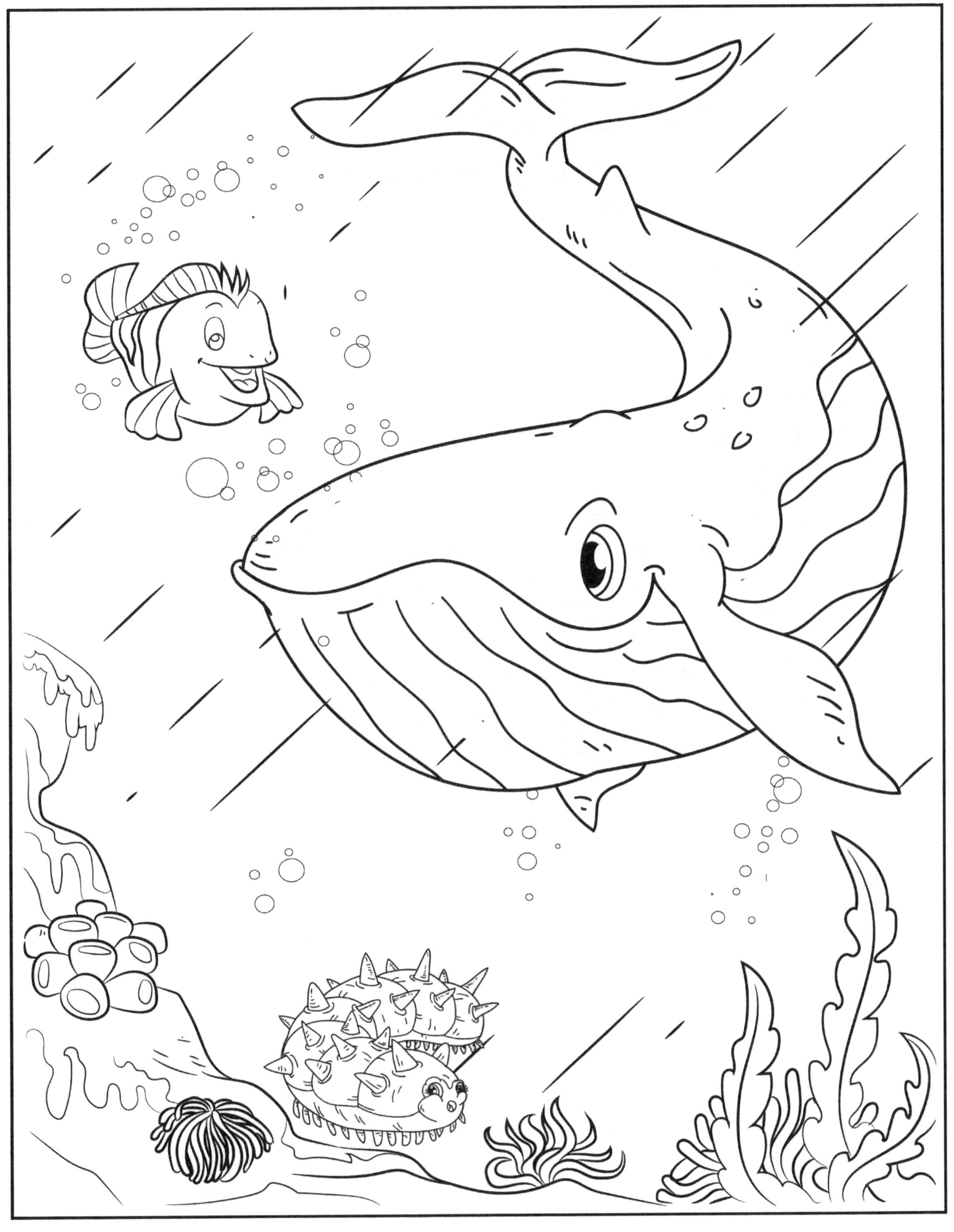

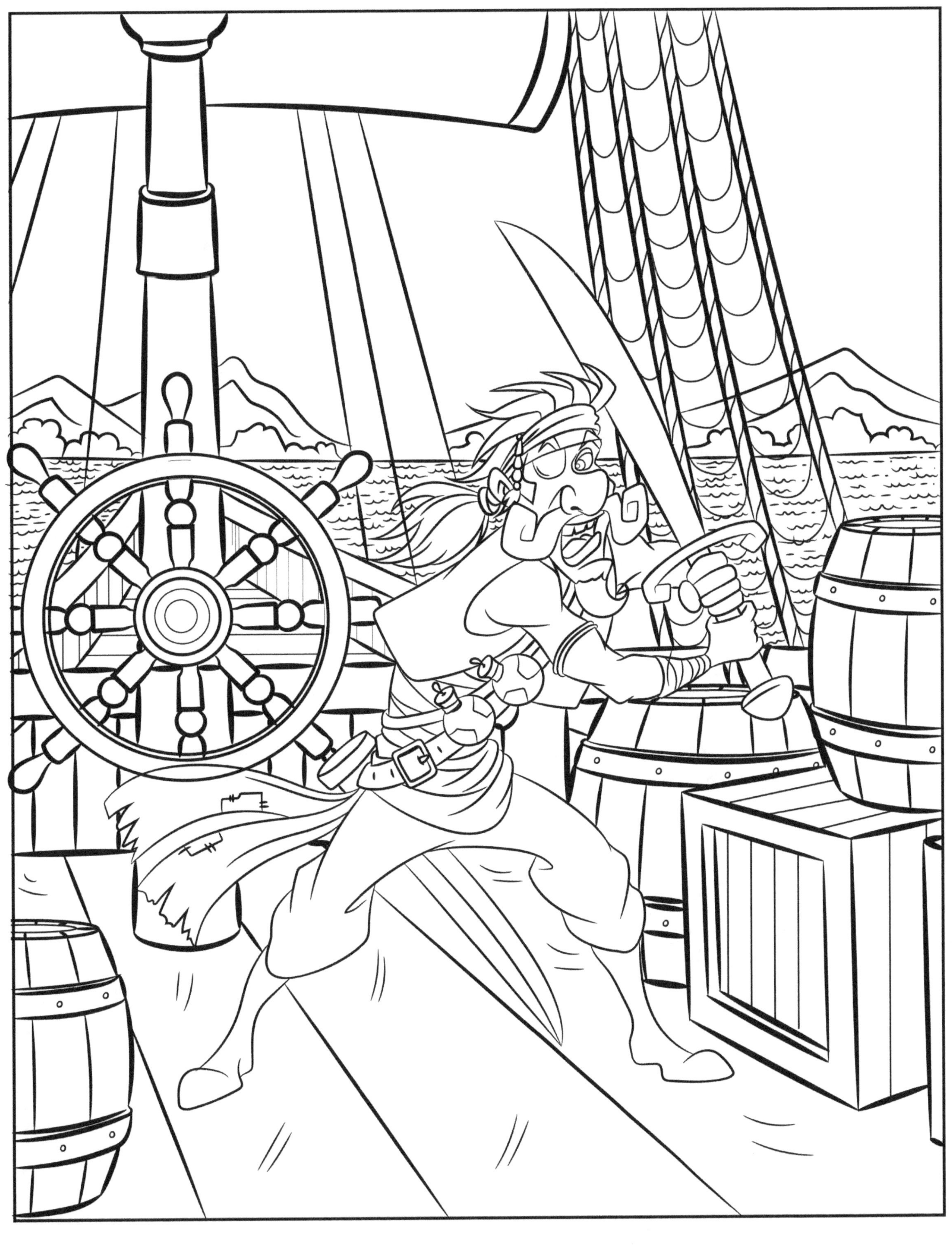

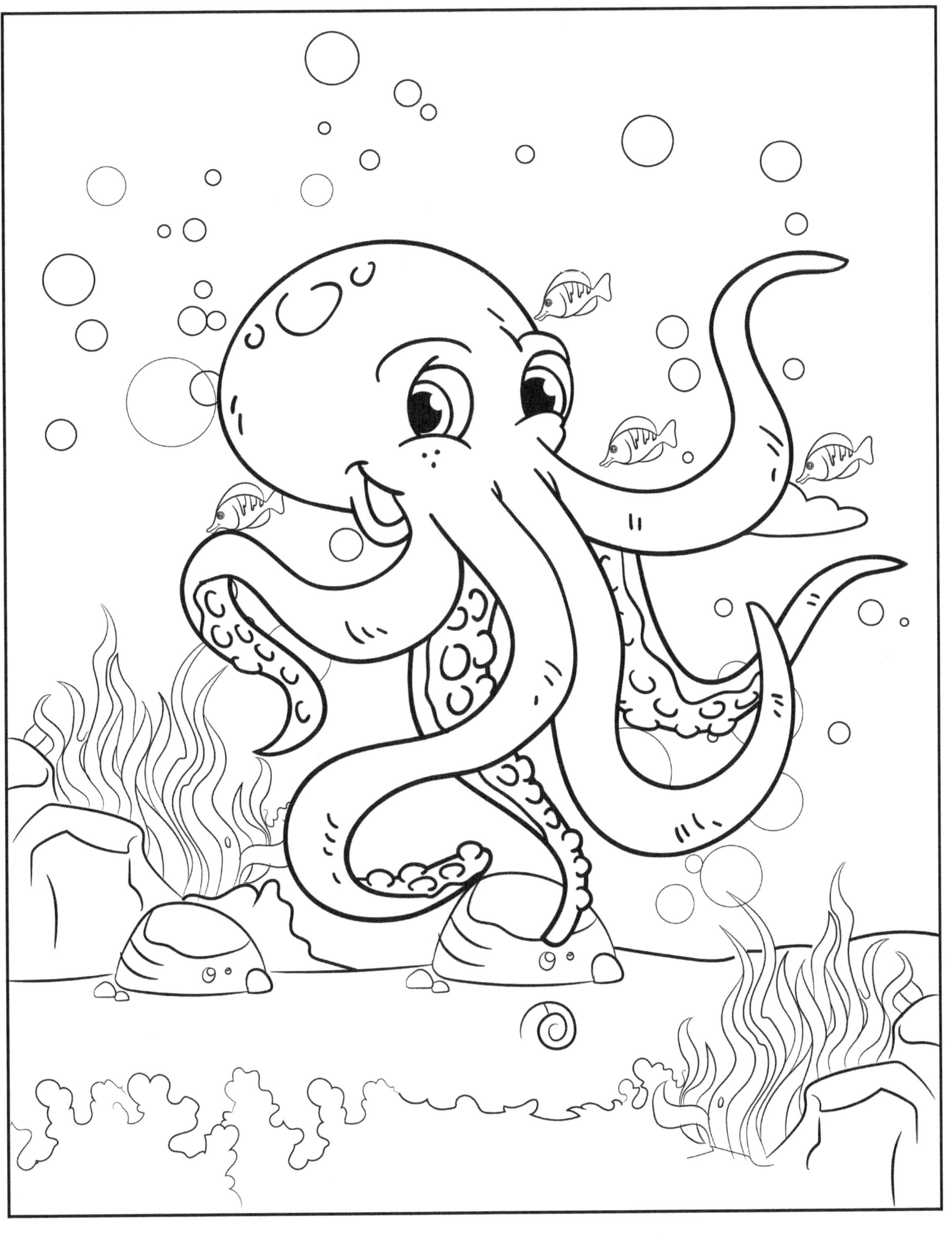

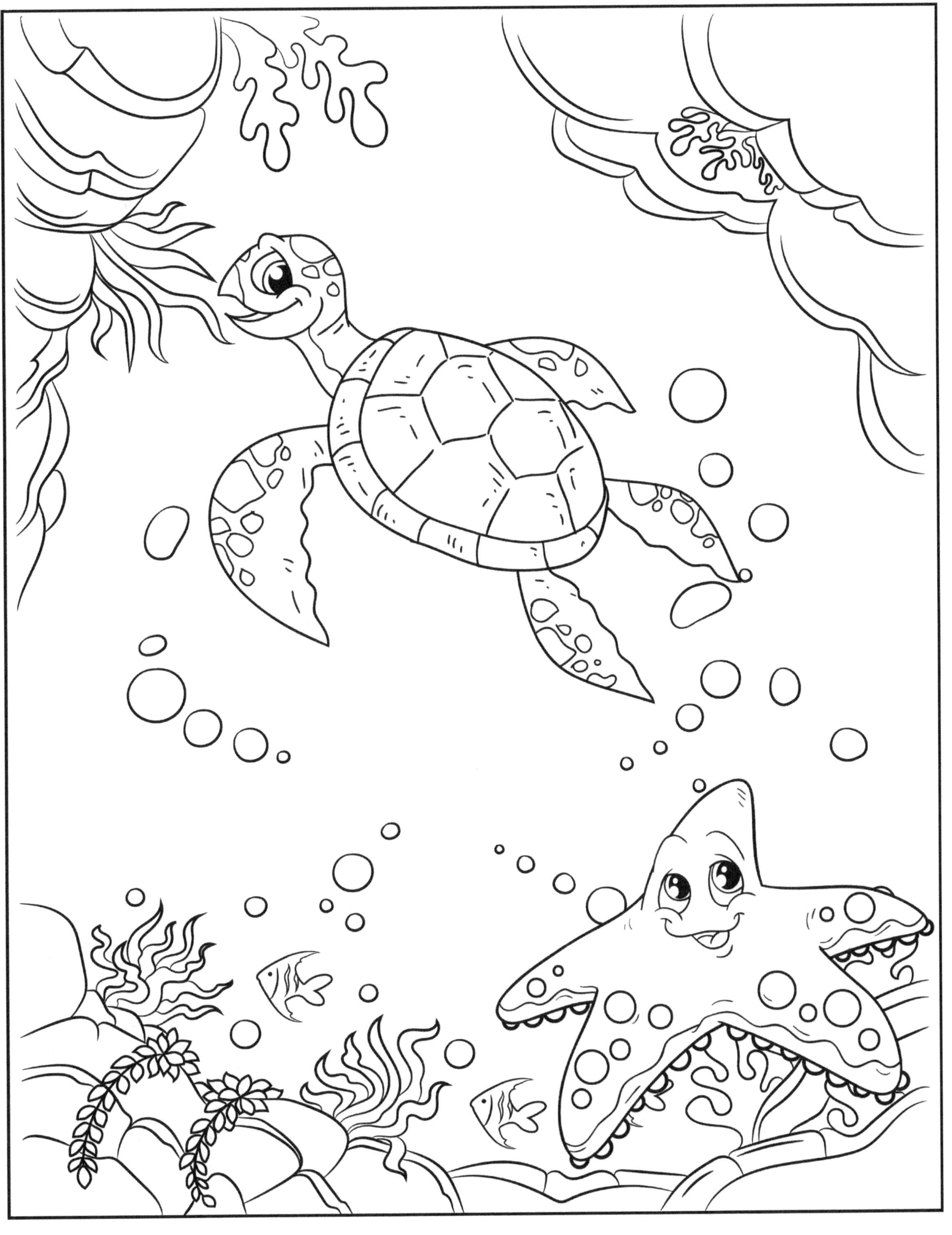

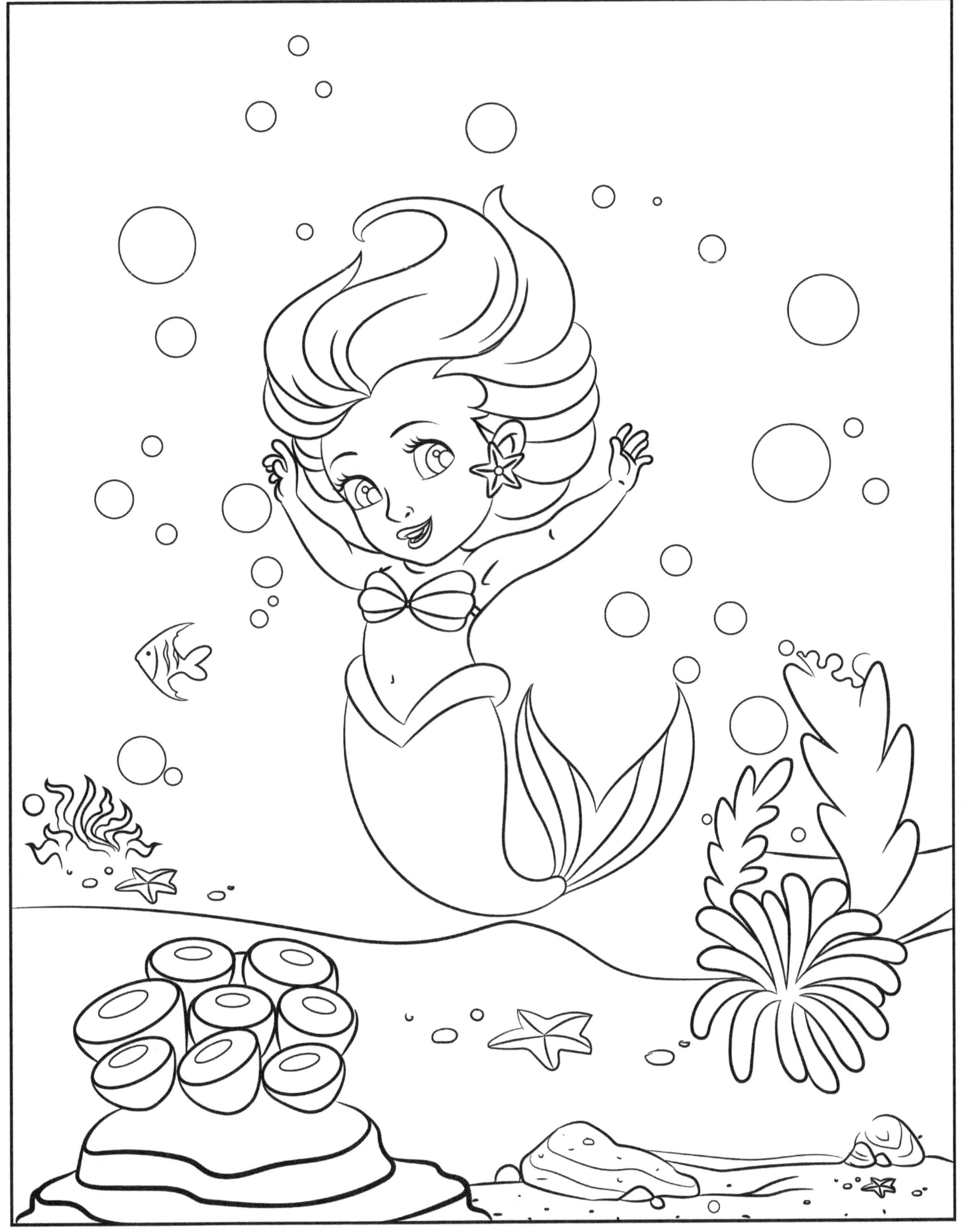

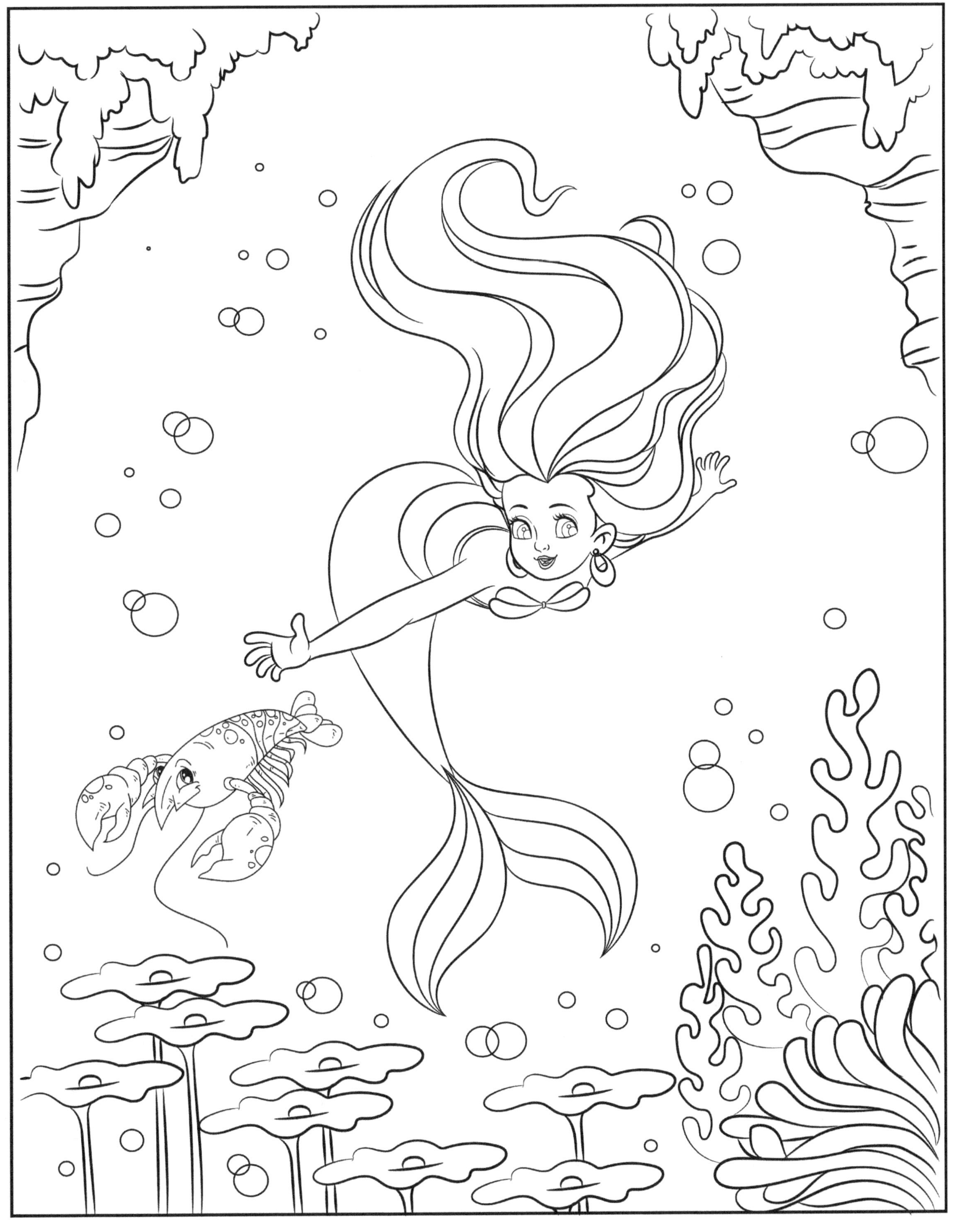

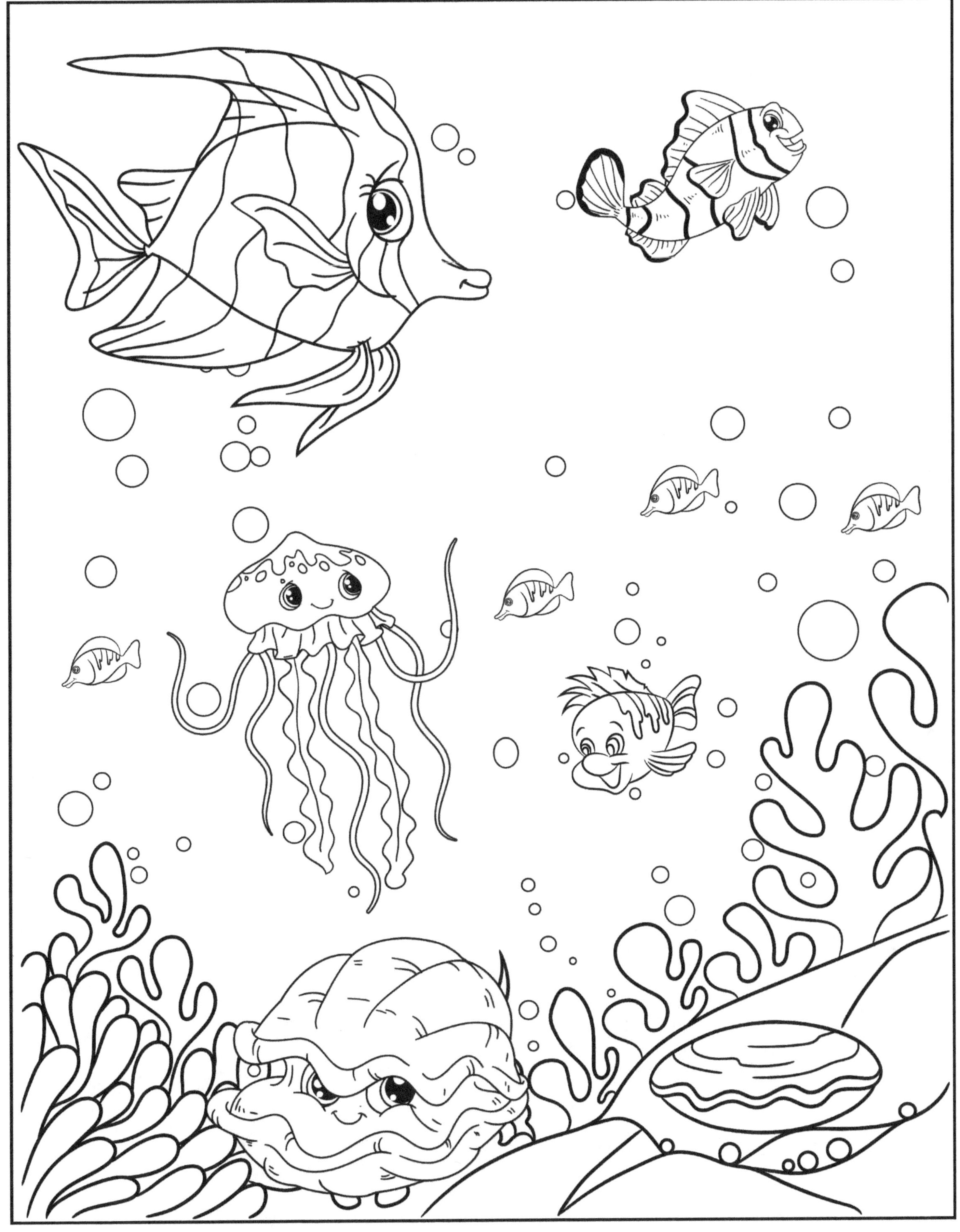

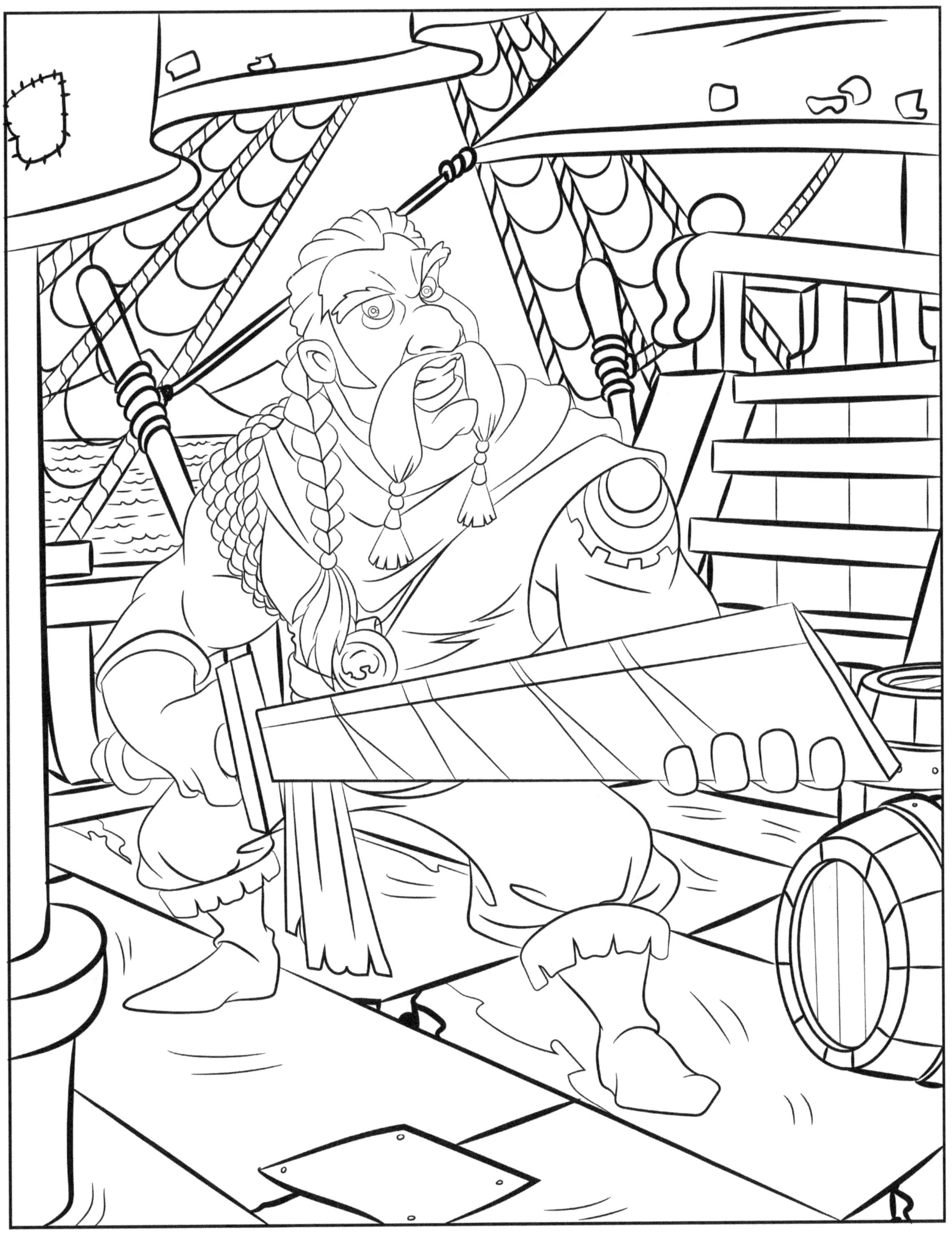

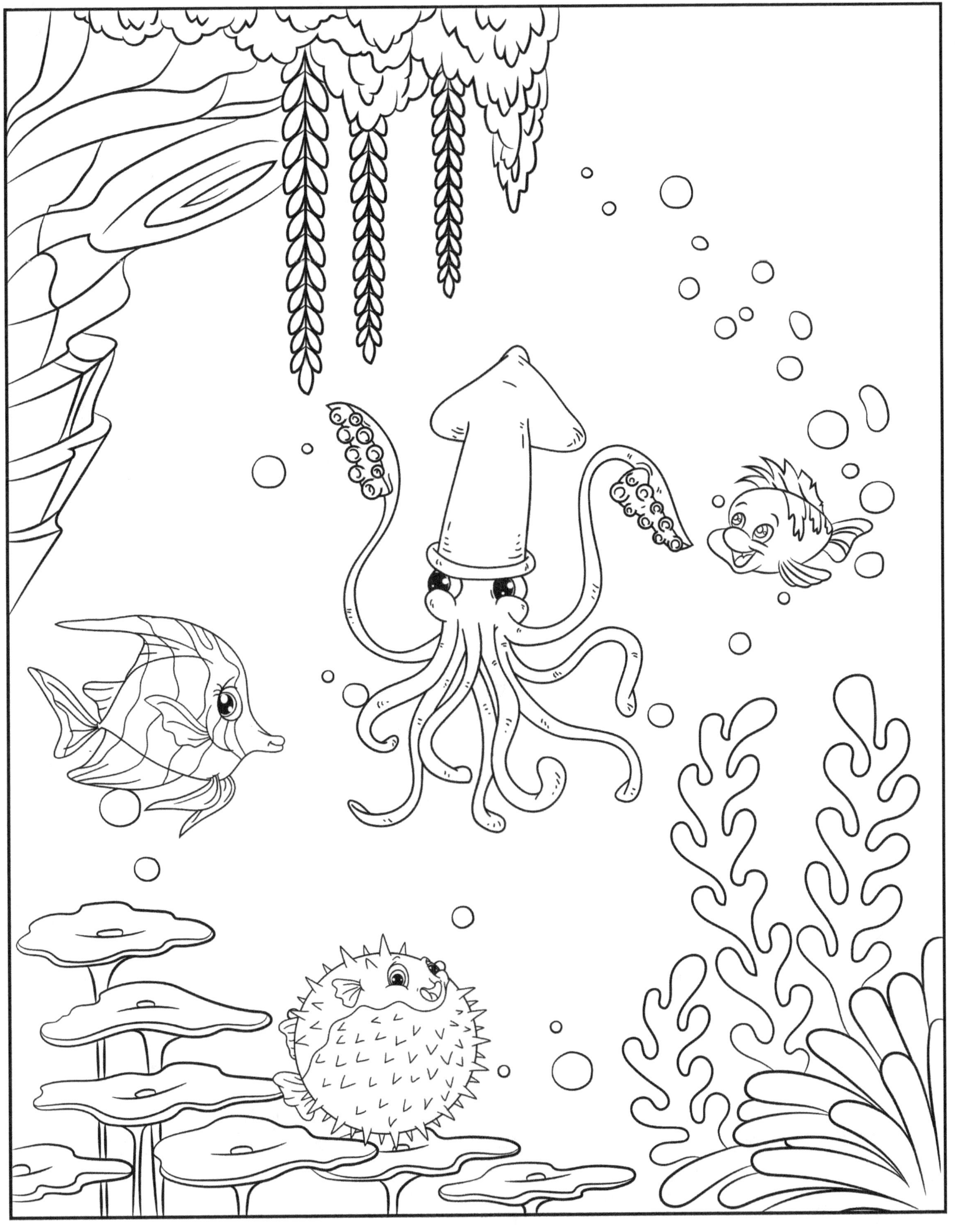

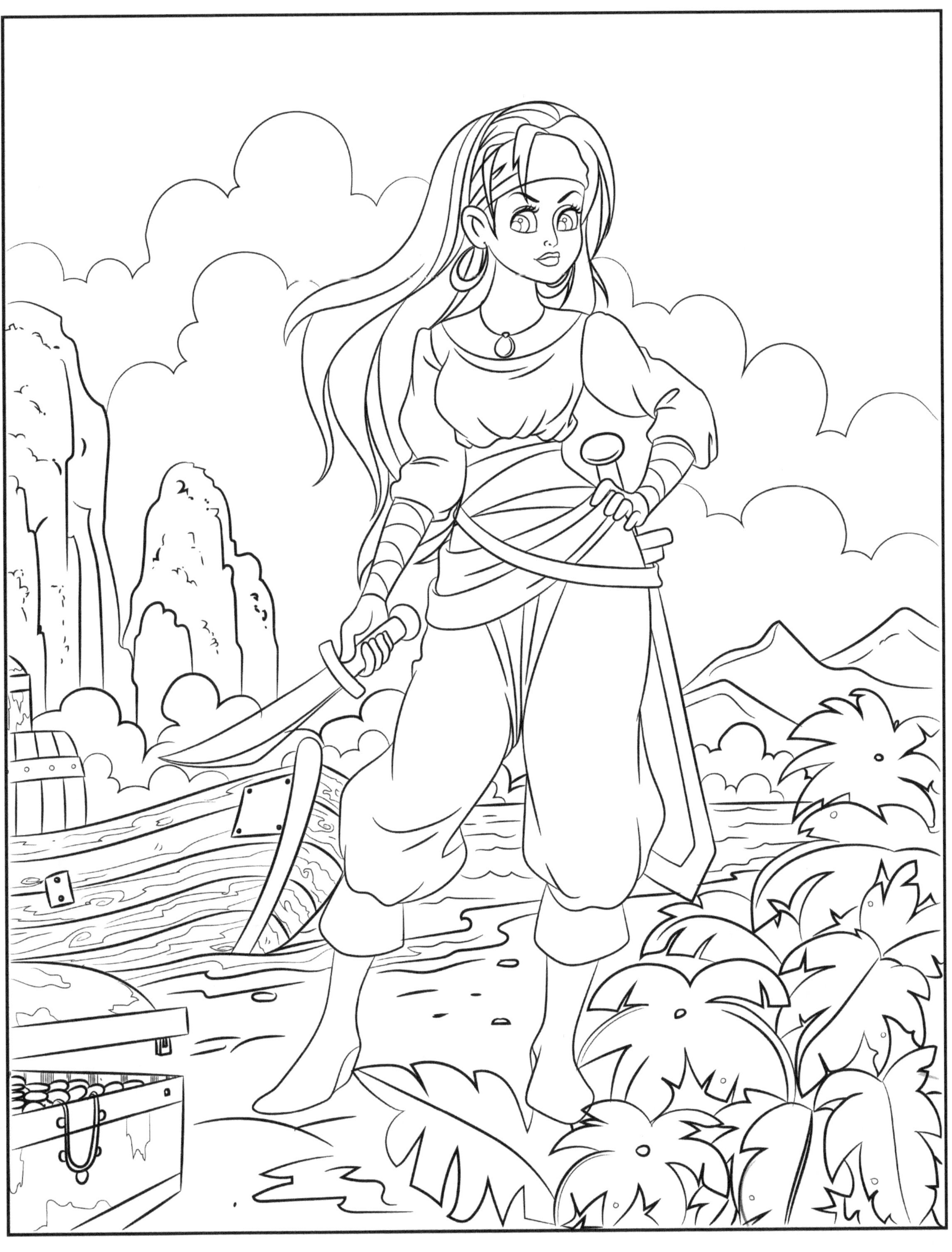

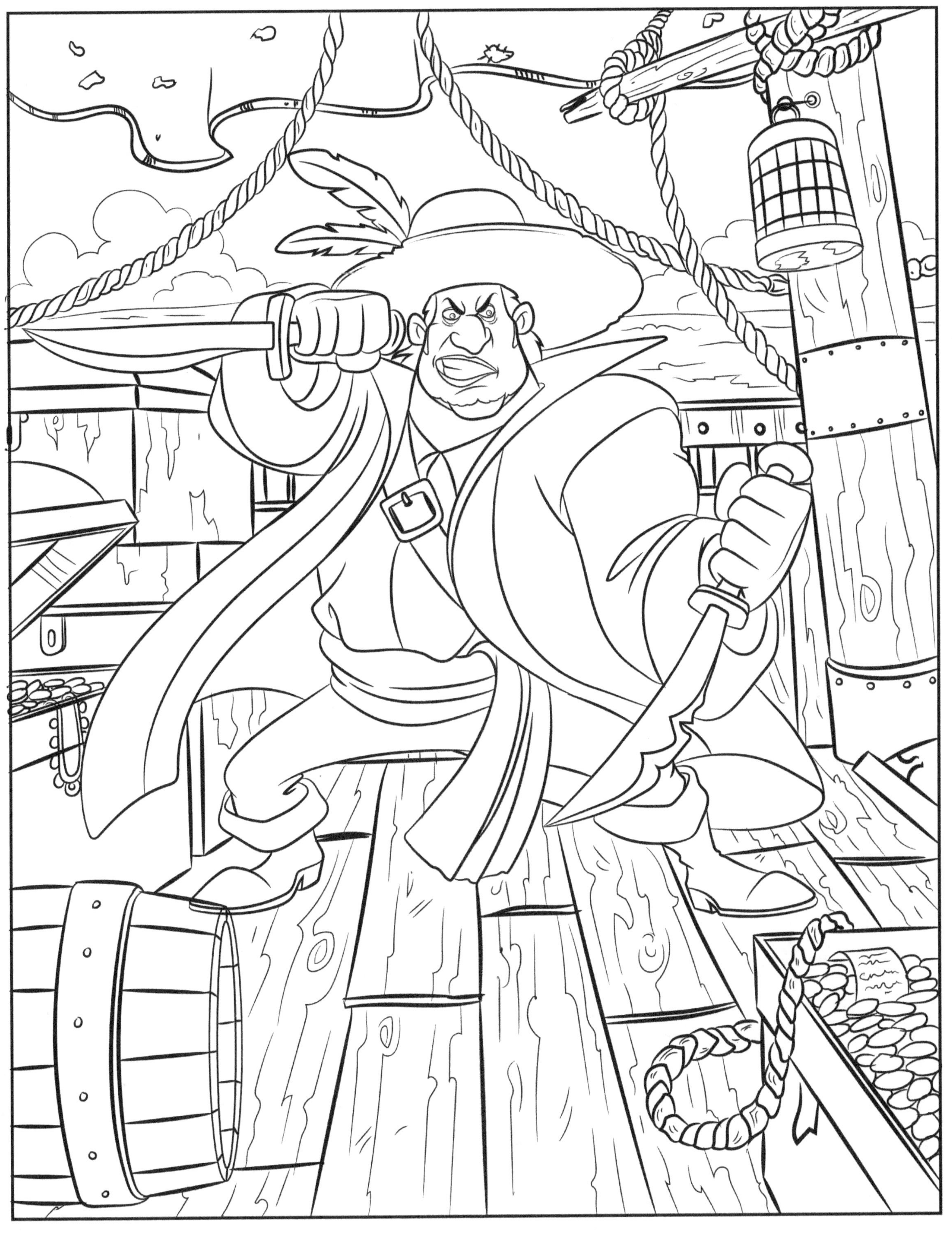

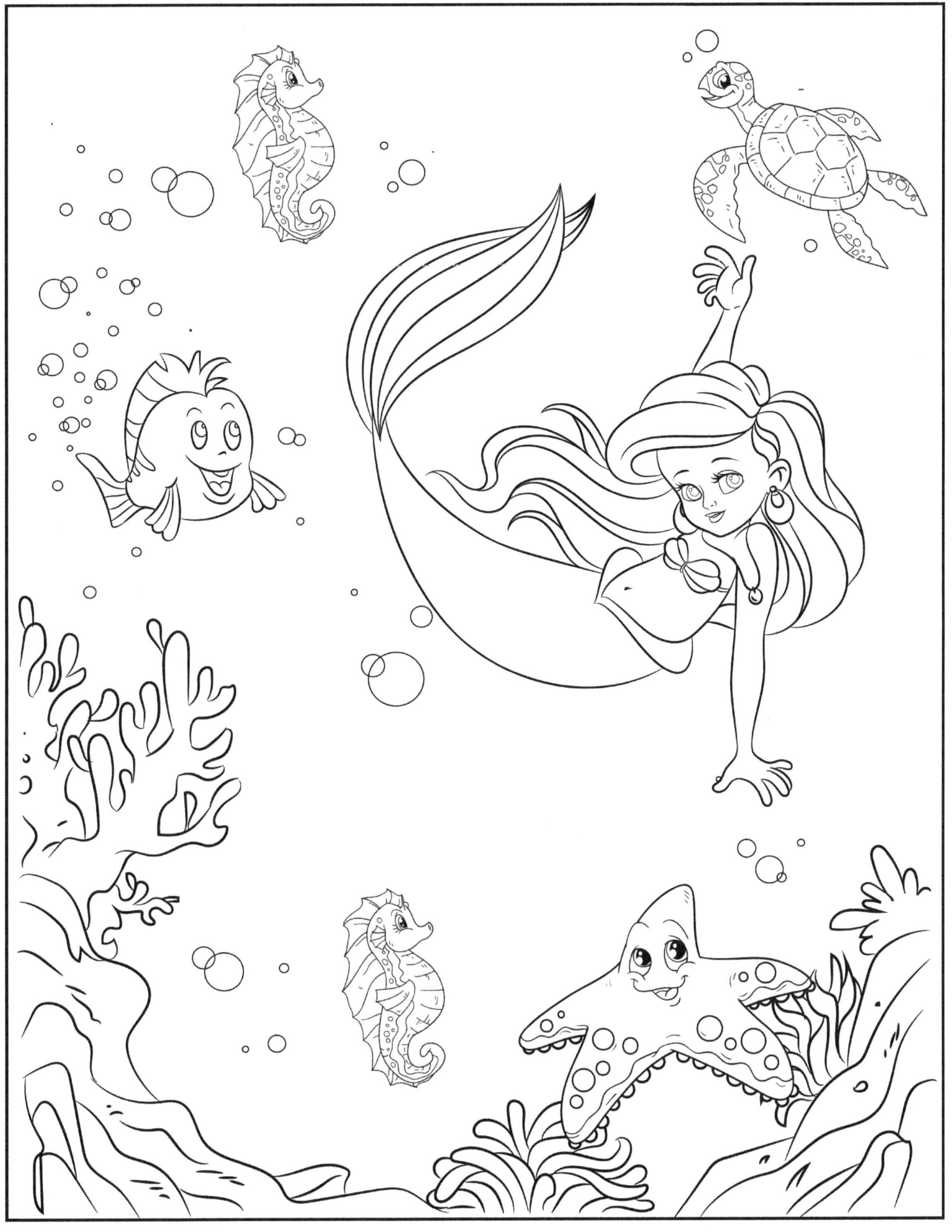

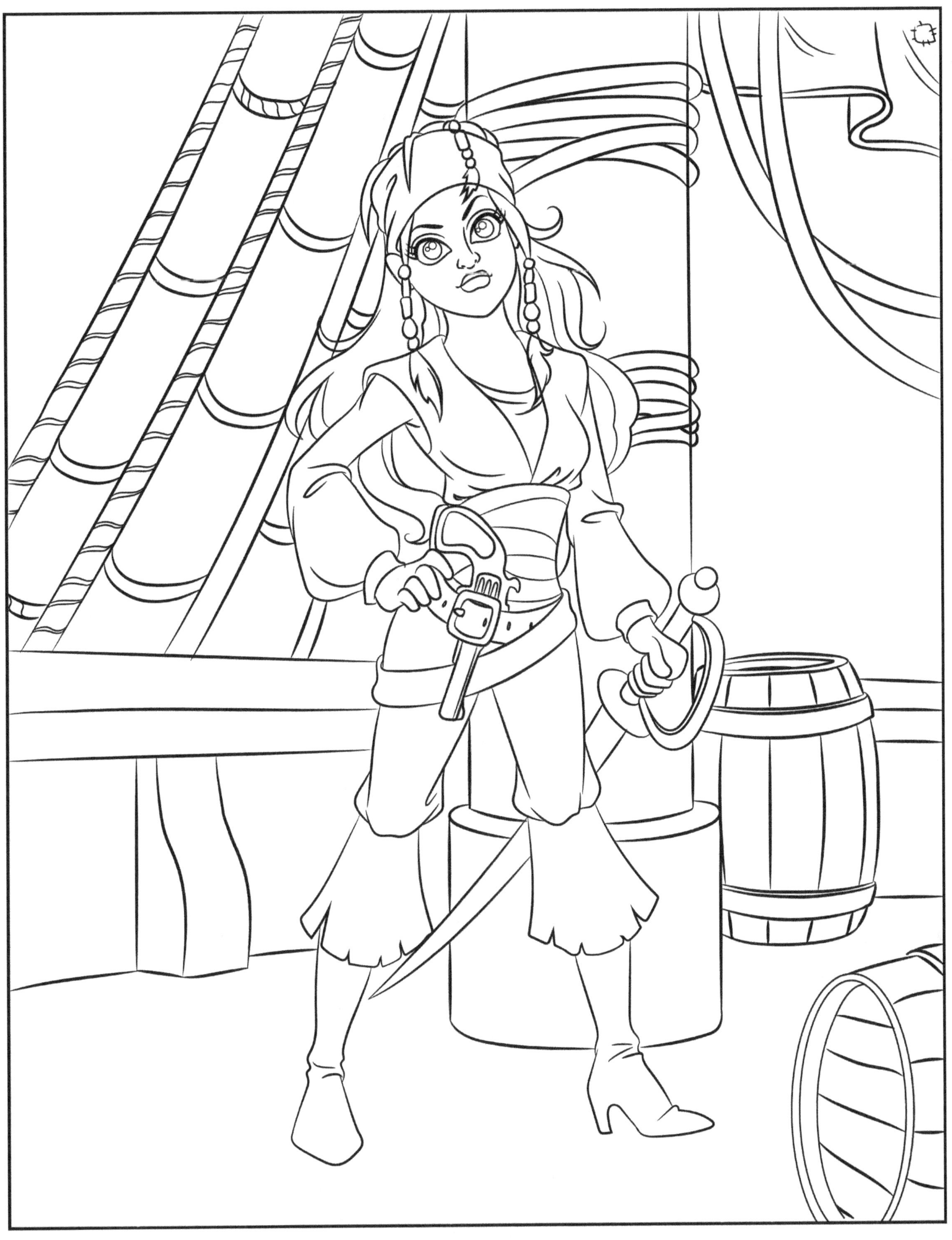

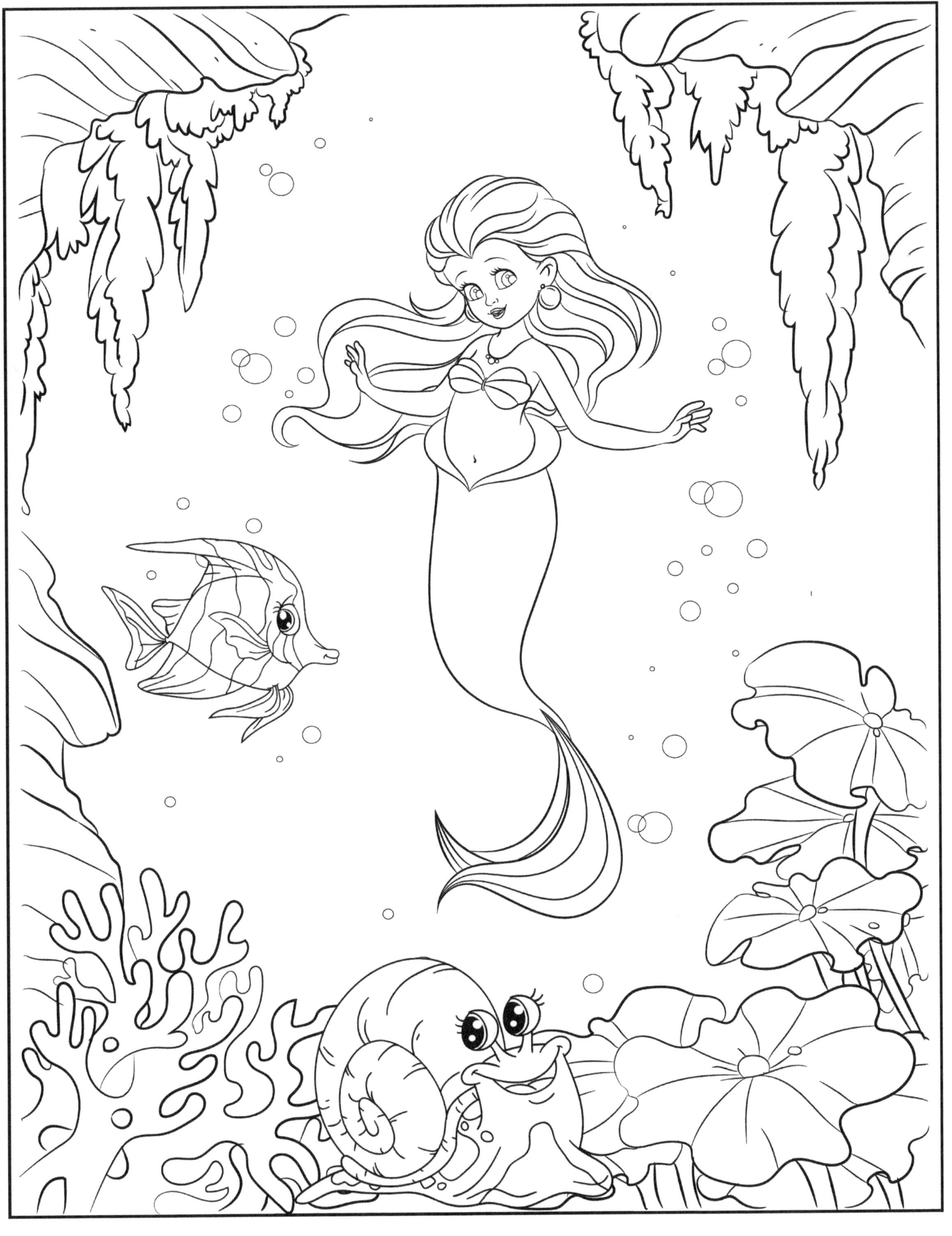

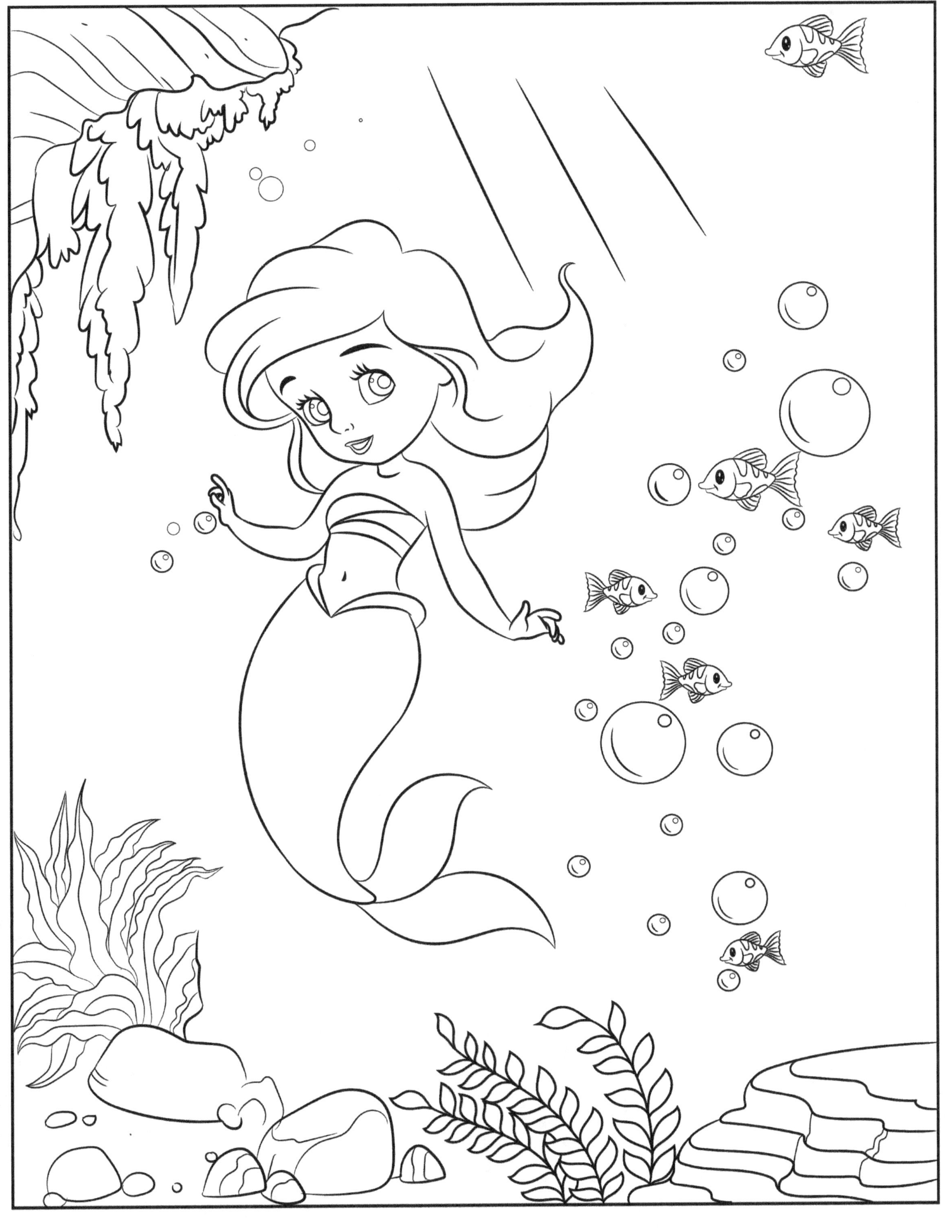

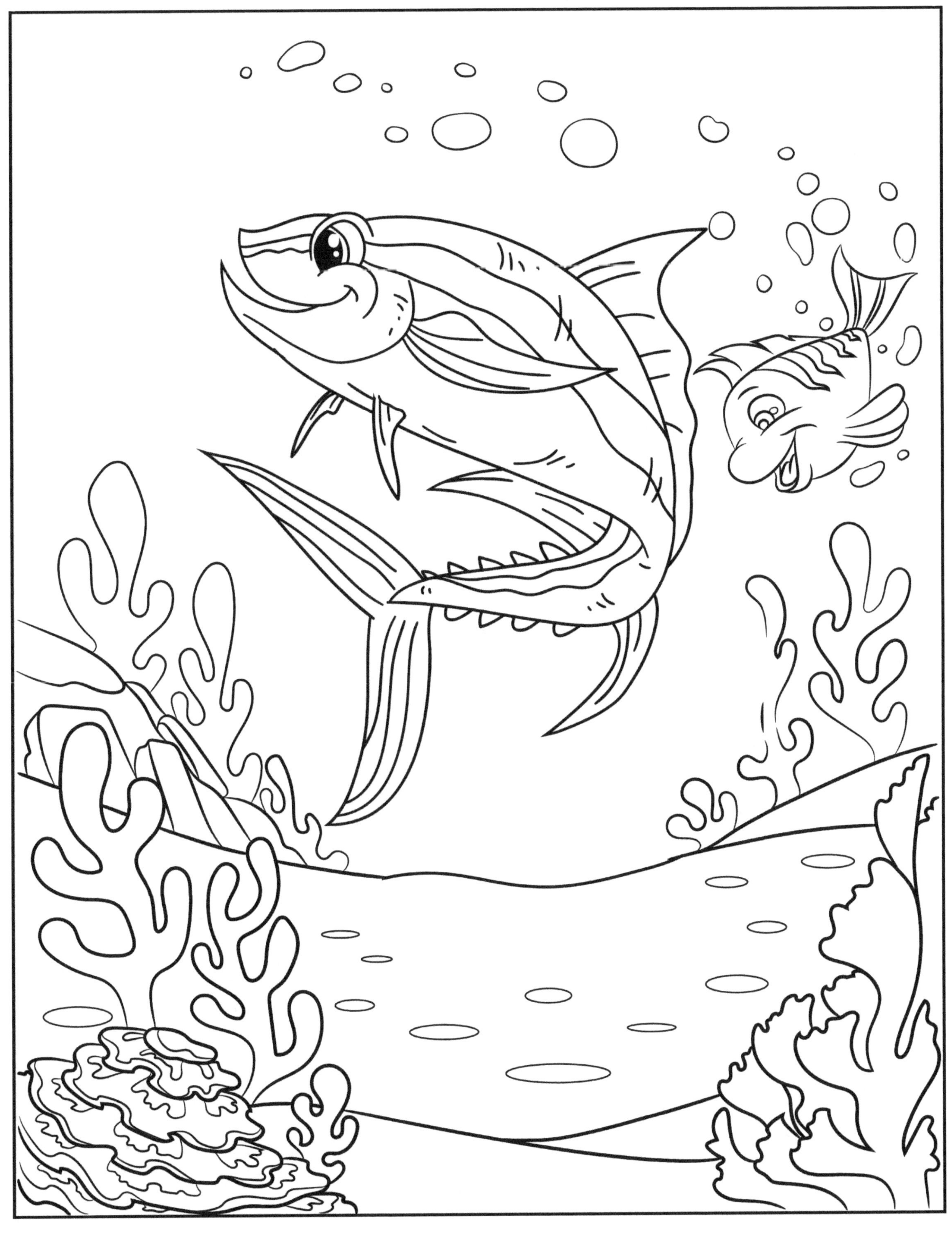

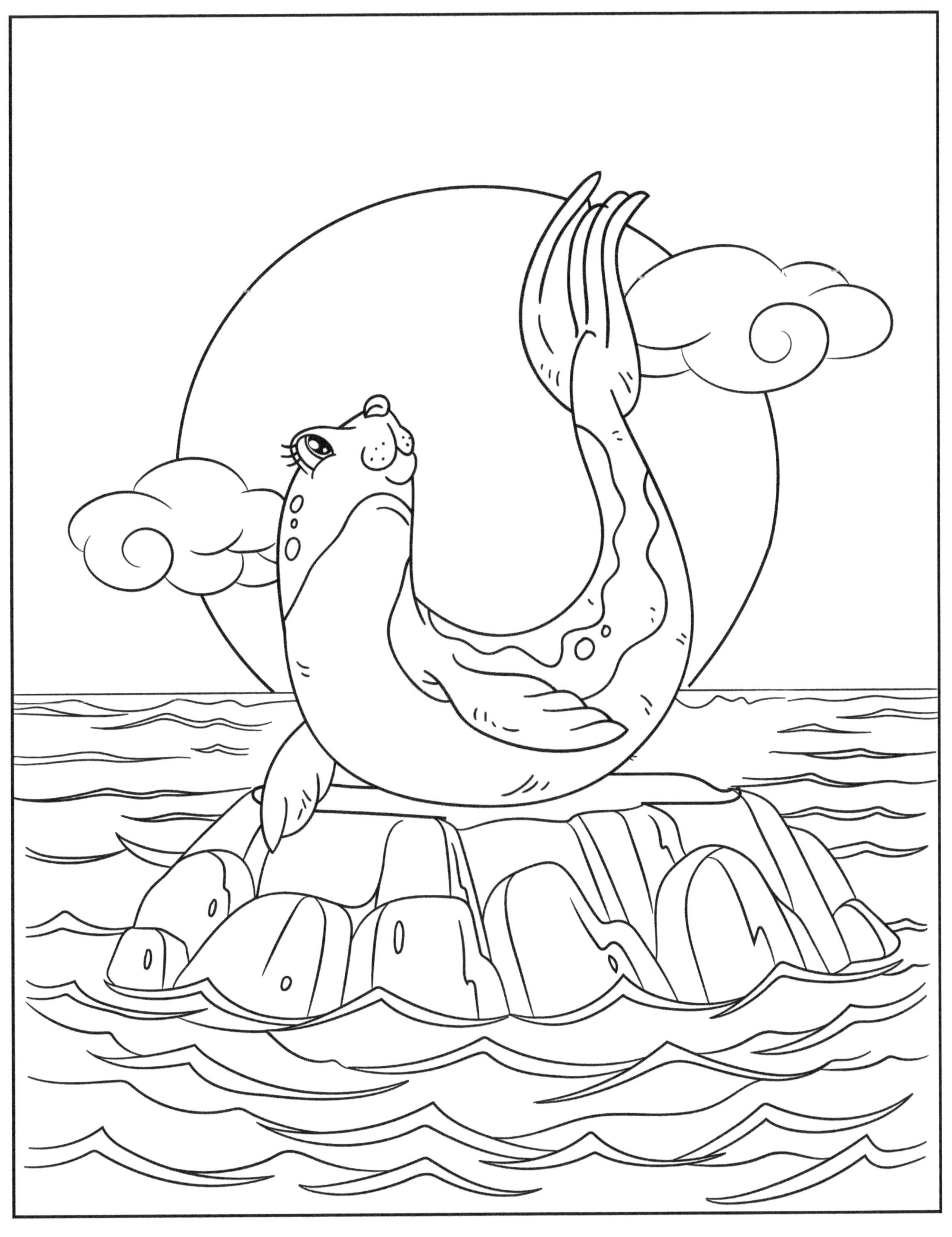

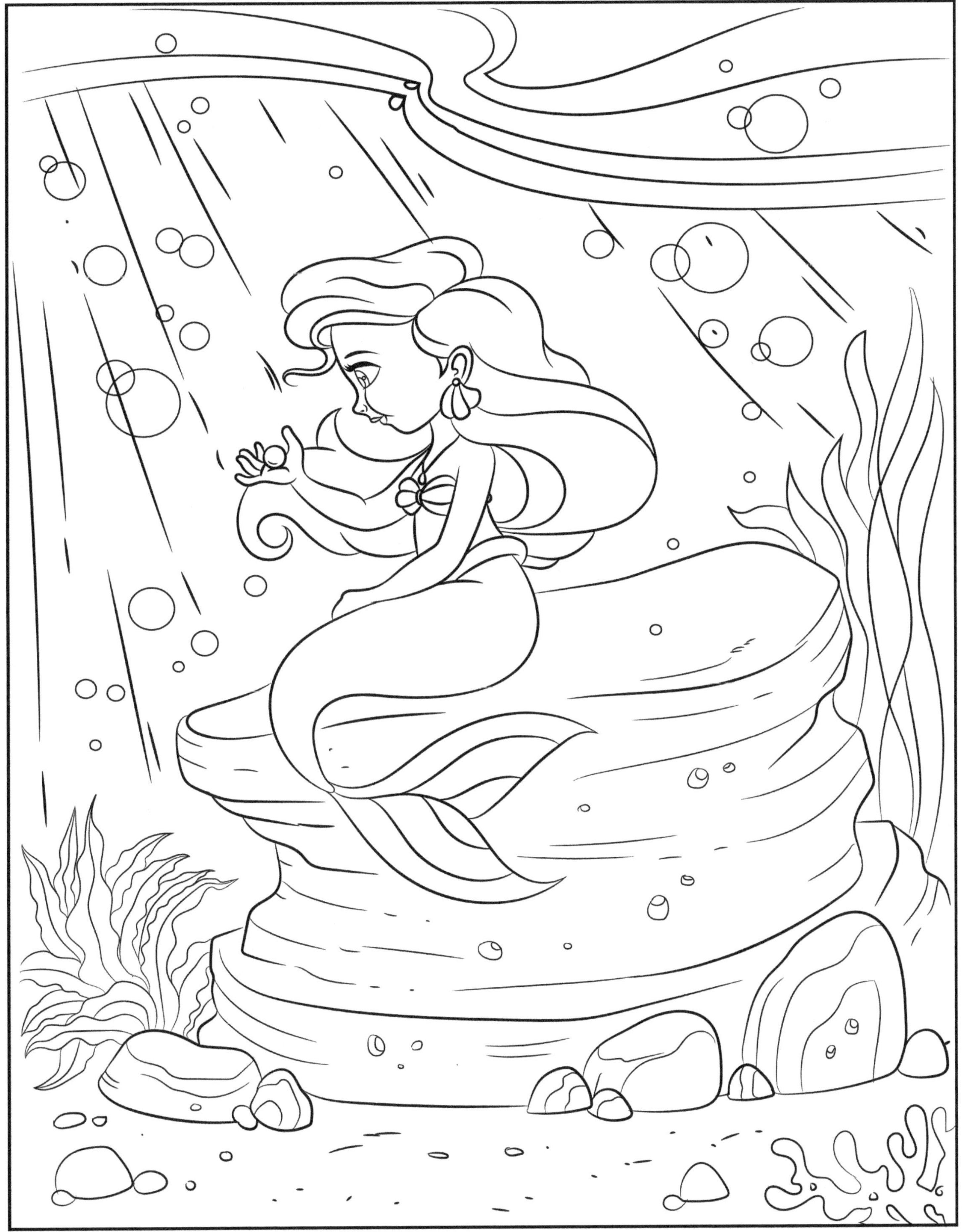

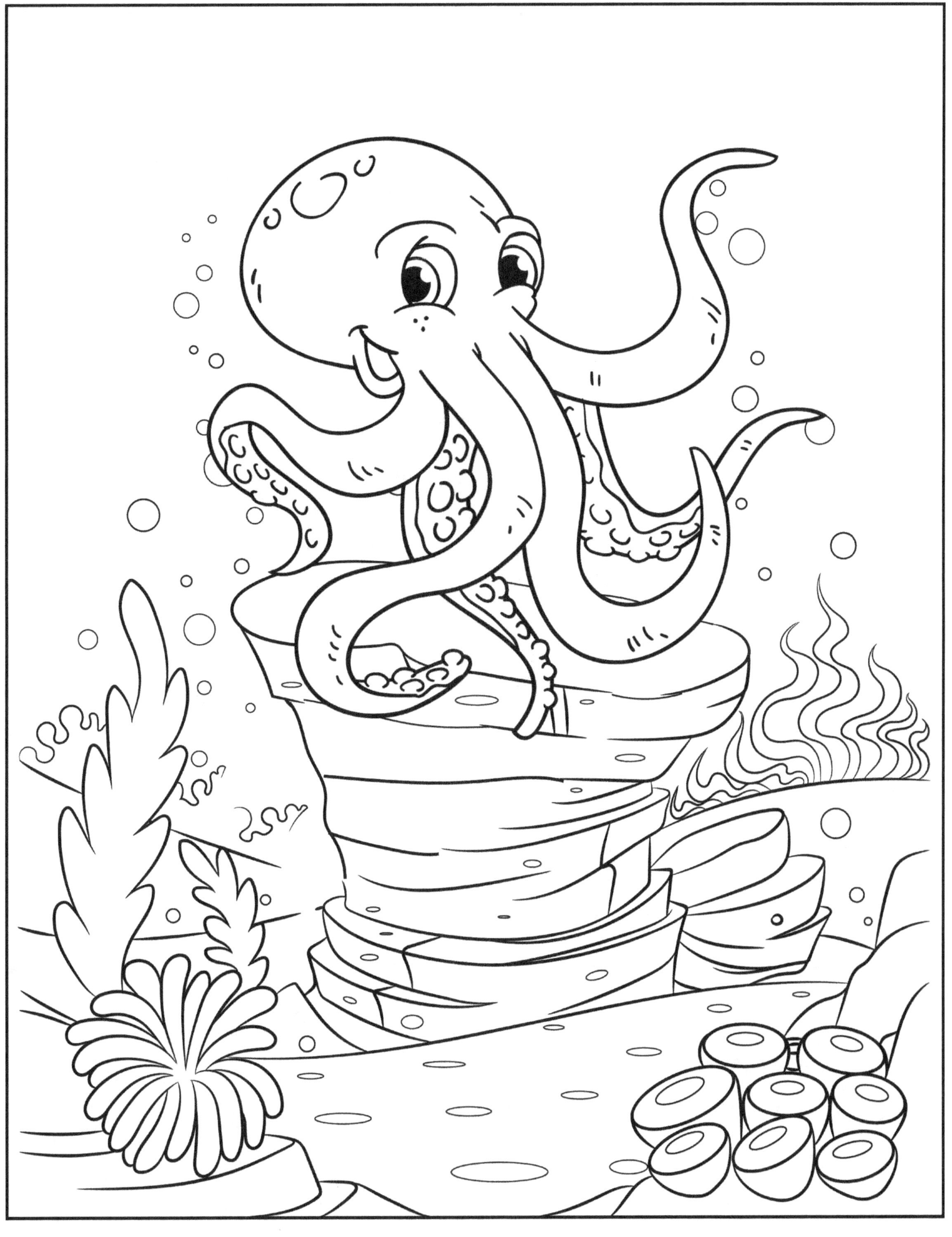

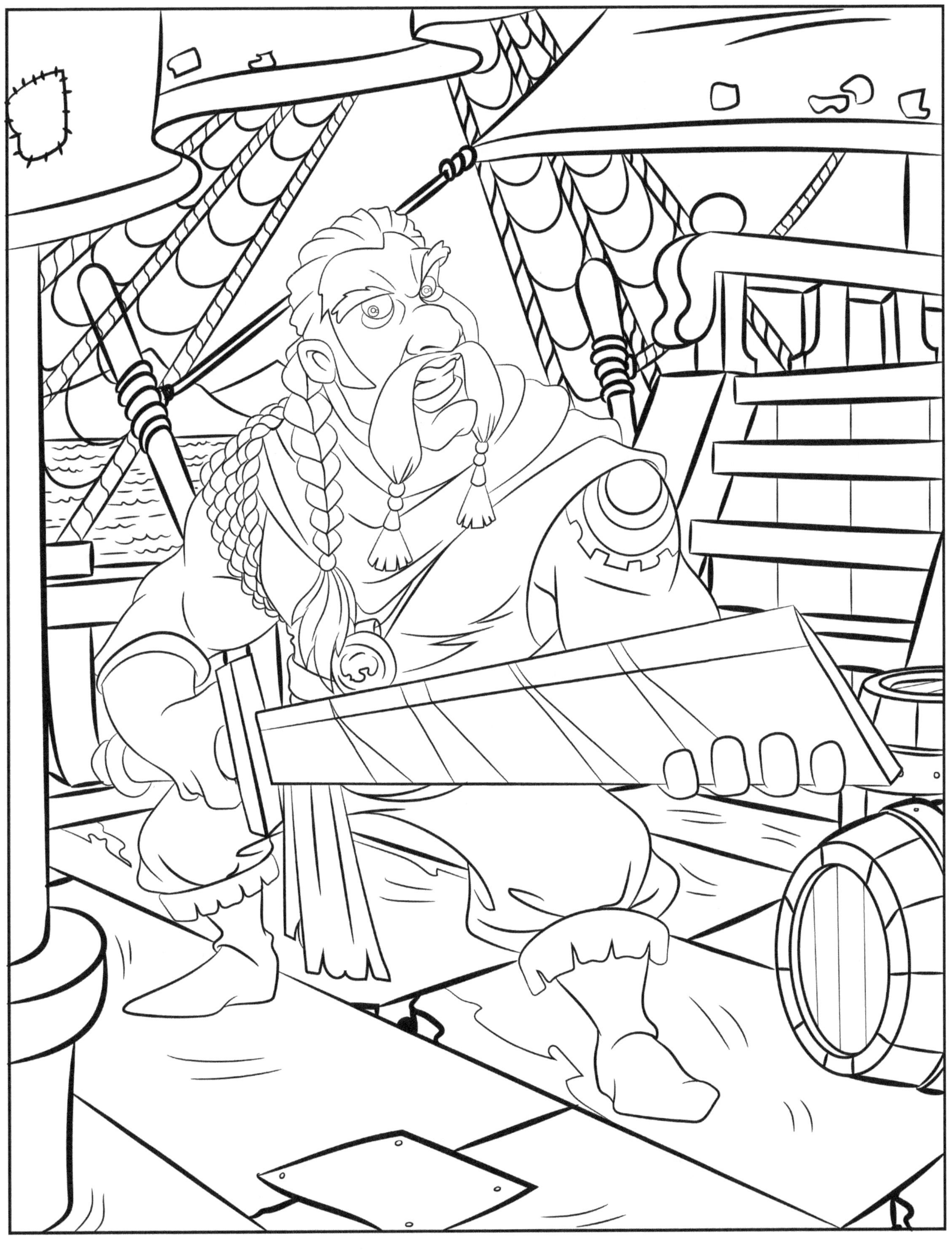